The DevOps Revolution
Disrupting the Status Quo – From IT Modernization
To Digital Competitiveness

The DevOps Revolution

Disrupting The Status Quo – From IT Modernization
to Digital Competitiveness

Philippe A. Abdoulaye

Knowledge Taken to You

From The Digital IT Academy™

Many of the designations used by manufacturers and sellers to distinguish their products are claimed as trademarks.

The author and publisher have taken care in the preparation of this book, but make no expressed or implied warranty of any kind and assume no responsibility for errors or omissions. No liability is assumed for incidental or consequential damages in connection with or arising out of the use of the information contained herein.

ISBN: 978-1-731-12302-2

The Digital IT Academy
3132 Calvary Drive – Suite 103
Raleigh, NC, 27604

www.itaasnow.com

To the memory of our Aunt, Catherine Auleley.

To my grandmother Julia Roger and brother Hugues-Christian Roger

Acknowledgements

The principles, assumptions, concepts, methodologies and recommendations developed in this book are the result of a long research.

They capitalize on the experience and skills gathered across a 20-year business transformation experience and six years advising on DevOps and Cloud Computing worldwide.

They're also the result of a long chain of support, first Thank you God.

Thank you to Michelle and Samuel, my mother Julienne Roger, and to my family for their patience.

I also thank Myriam L. Azizet for her golden friendship, Didier Ontchangalt for his constant support, the Abdoulaye family, the Roger Family, Romain Ogandaga and Max Rempano.

I can't forget Nicole Gakou, Florence Nang, Jean-Louis Guenego, Bertrand Mayesky, Martial Evina, Stephanie Carton, Michelle Gaillard, Claude Barrail, Antoni Ogonowski, Patrick Le Du, all of you for the fantastic moment we spent delivering IT transformation projects.

Special dedication to the Non-Governmental Organization (NGO) EDUCARE+ and her leader, the remarkable Aurelia Mombey for the fantastic contribution getting kids with disabled parents out of poverty via education.

Special thanks, always, to author, speaker and thought leader Joe McKendrick who, through his writings and vision, gave my career a fresh start.

Finally thank you to my partners, clients, and conference attendees, particularly Rackspace USA, Econocom France, BAIP Lithuania, XXL Solutions Switzerland, La Banque Postale Toulouse, EDF France, CNES France, Orange, and more.

Thank You All.

Contents

About this Book

Objective of this book

The purpose of this book is to help businesses adjust their DevOps implementation project to two major priorities:

- The organizational transformation of the business versus the competitive constraints of the disrupted markets created by Google, Amazon, Facebook, and Apple (GAFAs in the rest of the book)
- The monetization of their DevOps capability

Today's DevOps implementation practices are based on the belief that deploying more applications, cheaper, and faster will make the business competitive, profitable and likely to resist the GAFAs and the tough competitive environments they create.

An increasing number of surveys and case studies are showing that, this assumption is definitely false. Do you honestly think that to make your favorite business line profitable, the most important thing will be to deploy more software, cheaper, and faster? I hope you don't!

This book draws on the author's 20-year business and IT transformation experience improving companies' operational performance.

It's not the outlined summary of studies carried out by others or from publishers' points of view, the assumptions and recommendations presented in this book, result from feedback and knowledge capitalization, skills and practices acquired from real-life projects.

The intended audience for this book

This book is for CIOs, CTOs, CEOs, IT managers, Enteprise Architects, Project Managers, and all potential stakeholders involved in DevOps and cloud computing implementation projects.

People interested in understanding the impacts of the recent IT innovations on how companies do business will find substantial value in it.

Who this book is not intended for

If you're a professional programmer or a DevOps tools expert, this book isn't designed to be your primary resource. You may still decide to add it to your bookshelf, but you'll need other books that get into the details of topics as various as platform business models, digital service development, organizational restructuring, process reengineering, operational performance, design thinking, and change management.

To make your reading and understanding easy, key words, concepts, methodologies out of the IT world are linked and redirected to websites providing elaborated information.

Having said that, the book may help you view today's DevOps implementation practices with a critical eye and align yours or those of your clients with the requirements of today's disrupted markets.

Introduction

The massive hypes surrounding the recent technology innovations — Microservices, Containers, Cloud Computing, Artificial Intelligence (AI), Internet of Things (IoT), Big Data Analytics, Blockchain — hides the undeniable fact that today's IT practices are reaching an inflection point.

Many changes in today's markets advocate in favor of a more effective approach to leverage technology to help companies solve the business problems they face.

The irruption of Google, Amazon, Facebook, Apple (GAFAs) in all industries and the disrupted markets they create have raised new competitive challenges; the CIO's historical conventional wisdom that, *"deploying more applications, cheaper, and faster is what matters"* isn't enough to meet them.

To survive and thrive, businesses need more than " *putting in the hands of their staff, these recent sophisticated IT tools."*

They must take control of their markets by continuously delivering innovations to turn their competitive environments in their favor. That's what's meant by being a market disruptor.

DevOps is seen as the solution that'll help your company meet the challenges of the rising digital competition. I totally agree with that. However, problems remain with several grey areas.

DevOps adoption is accelerating, the promised business benefits still don't show up

As a recommended TechRepublic's survey clarifies it in, "Why 78% of Organizations Fail to Get DevOps Right," despite its increasing adoption, businesses still don't see the promised business benefits of DevOps.

The only things they get is, a significant improvement of their IT department's performance and never, the help they expect to survive the GAFA's competition.

Nine West Holdings, The Bon-Ton Stores, Toys R Us, Remington, Southeastern Grocers, Tops Markets and recently Sears, victims of their industry's *digital disruption*, they all went bankrupt.

Why are all these bankruptcies happening? you might be asking. I see five reasons:

1. A misconception of the notion of digital disruption and how to prevent its impacts on the business

2. The IT department's misunderstanding of the notion of business value and how to create it
3. The erroneous IT department's belief that applications are the primary drivers of business value
4. The implementation of the recent IT innovations are disconnected from any digital business strategy
5. And more importantly, the challenge of translating DevOps culture into a tangible business capability

Disrupting your market is the primary business challenge, DevOps as implemented today doesn't help

The digital disruptions that are kicking companies out of business are misunderstood in the IT community.

The reason is, blinded by the widespread illusion that technology can fix any business problem, the IT community doesn't see that the stake for business lines is to meet the challenges raised by the proliferating tech startups and the GAFA, which take advantage of their platform business model and the expansion of the network economy onto markets, if not entire industries.

Patrick Debois, godfather of the DevOps movement, always says DevOps is a human problem, Damon Edwards co-creator of the DevOps CAMS concept—Culture, Automation, Measurement, Sharing—said, it's a management problem, in this book I add, it's also a competitive matter.

The IT community including certain DevOps experts, ignore the business line expectations, they resist the changes

While the challenge is to run the business with a market disruptor mindset, IT leaders and their IT service providers offer to massively deliver more applications, cheaper and faster as if, it was enough to meet the innovation, responsiveness, and customer experience excellence challenges.

The IT department's tool-focused mindset is a problem, it confines IT to the limited role of IT tools and infrastructure supplier.

By stressing IT applications as the primary competitiveness drivers, the IT department misses the point that is, the organizational transformation of the business, its structures, processes, and staff adaptation to the constraints and requirements of disrupted markets.

It's false and even illusory to believe that applications as sophisticated as they are, deployed massively at the speed of light, will dispense companies from reviewing their calcified processes, structures, and governance.

The notion of business value is overused in IT including in the DevOps community – it's an important failure factor of DevOps implementation

The issue of business value in the IT department and even within the entire IT community is a problem, it deserves to be clarified as there are so many misunderstandings.

Claims such as, "*Migrating the IT infrastructure to the cloud will increase business wealth*" or "*Deploying continuous deployment infrastructure will increase revenue*" raise questions as to how the IT department understands the notion of business value and how to create it.

Business value is simply the revenue your company generates from selling its products and services. Arguing that migrating IT to the cloud or deploying DevOps automation tools alone will result in value doesn't make sense.

Just to remind, value—the company's revenue—results from the combined actions of your company's key functions including Strategy, Marketing, Sales, Post Sales, Project Management (PMO), and of course, IT operations. "*Technology alone is enough to create value*" is something that must be twisted, it's false.

These DevOps failure factors show that, creating business value is the primary concerns of your business lines, it should not be confined in software development issues.

The fact of the matter is, business value creation is a cross-functional process that starts with the identification of customer expectations, moves on with translating customer expectations into innovative and profitable service ideas, and ends with service development, rollout, and continuous customer experience improvement.

IT vendors' marketing hypes are a problem, they're the primary failure factor of DevOps implementation

DevOps vendors' biggest mistake is, they took software development and deployment out of the overall business value creation process and are selling it as the new business value creation paradigm.

In other words, DevOps vendors are telling businesses that, to resist Google, Amazon, Facebook, Apple, and Walmart, the most important thing is to automate their software development and deployment activities with Jenkins, Chef, Puppet, and Docker, and that, value will be automatically generated.

Are they serious?

This oversimplification of the value creation process has a damaging impact on businesses; it prevents them from taking the important decision to properly adapt the way they work to the new competition requirements.

The challenge of translating the abstract notion of DevOps culture into a tangible business capability

The claim that DevOps is primarily a culture, not a technology or a software development framework and not even a role causes confusion in many experts' mind.

The question many businesses have been asking that, DevOps experts including renowned thought leaders don't dare to answer is, *"How do you convert DevOps culture into a tangible business asset?"*

The answer is never given because it transcends IT tool concerns; it relates to business transformation matters and demands knowledge today's techies aren't skilled with—operational model, agile transformation, organizational restructuring, interaction optimization, creativity, tactical sense, business understanding.

Inability to convert DevOps culture into a tangible business asset is definitely one of the top reasons of DevOps implementation failure.

Why the solutions in this book are the answers businesses have been expecting for years

The vision and approach in this book explain DevOps through three fundamental concepts that have revolutionized the way business value is created and managed. They come from Harvard's strategy professor Michael Porter and management guru Henry Mintzberg:

- The **Value Chain** (relates to DevOps' notion of Value Stream) addressed in this book as the business operational model
- The **Five Forces** model which helps to understand the whys and wherefores of industry changes
- The **Organizational Culture** (relates to the notion of DevOps culture) introduced by Henry Mintzberg as the collective wisdom, which comes from lessons learned as people adapt and survive together over time.

The business operational model is a framework that helps to spot, analyze, and optimize the added-value interactions your company should leverage to create value.

For each interaction, the required staff and skills, processes and practices, values and behaviors, and of course IT tools and infrastructure are clearly specified.

You got it, the business operational model is the most strategic, the most important piece of your company; it's where business wealth is created.

Most DevOps implementations fail to deliver the expected business value because they don't take into account the transformation of the company's operational model.

The perspectives, concepts, tools, and recommendations in this book are helping several Fortune 500 companies reinvent themselves and boost their business. The ambition is to do the same for your company and your career.

Philippe A. Abdoulaye
Founder & CEO
ITaaS Now & The Digital IT Academy
https://www.itaasnow.com

1. How DevOps Could Have Revamped Toys "R" Us

The story you're about to read and its recommendations are real; they contrast with what you have heard so far about digital transformation and DevOps implementation.

Its objective is to convince you about that the time to go digital is now; it's about transforming your business, not only IT; and to do it you'll have to implement DevOps entirely.

This chapter covers:

- How failing to address market disruptions takes to bankruptcy
- Transforming the business is prerequisite to survive and thrive
- DevOps is the problem, its misconception is the problem

How Failing to Address Market Disruption Takes to Bankruptcy

In September, Toys R Us, one of the world's largest toys store chains, filed for bankruptcy protection.

A better understanding of how disruption in the retail industry impacted the company would have helped to prevent its downfall and to reinvent its business model.

For example, providing Toys 2.0 (a generic term referring to a new generation of toys built on cloud, mobility, IoT and AI technologies) gaming services could have helped the company survive.

Shifting to Toys 2.0 demands a revolution in thinking, vision, practice and value that business leaders, CIOs and IT vendors haven't done yet.

They must forget the obsolete notion that technology and speed determine business success. Adopting paradigms that stress innovation and solve competitive constraints is the safest path toward fast and durable revenue.

Transforming the business is a prerequisite to survive and thrive

The biggest problem Toys R Us faced was the fact that consulting firms and IT vendors either didn't understand the challenge as an digital disruption issue — or if they did, they improperly addressed it.

Let's clarify: To tackle your industry's disruption, you must adapt your business model including the set of interactions, staff and skills, processes and practices, beliefs and values and infrastructure and tools used across your company to generate revenue.

Digital disruption is the challenge, and DevOps through its many assets is the unique business capability companies need to quickly transform and win their digital battles.

DevOps is the Solution, Its Misconception is the Problem

The problem, as Alan Shimel, founder, CEO and editor in chief of DevOps(dot)com, puts it is, *"While so many companies have already started to use DevOps or planning to use DevOps and related methodologies soon, there is only a small percentage of companies that are end-to-end DevOps. This means there is still tremendous opportunity in bringing DevOps to market."*

How should have Toys R Us leveraged DevOps to tackle its industry's disruption? Why did investing in that global digital e-commerce platform prove insufficient? How well did they transform their business model? How would have implementing DevOps 100 percent helped to overcome Amazon and Walmart competition?

The following chapters provide the precious answers.

What You Must Keep in Mind

Market disruptions aren't fantasies invented by marketers trying to make big money; they're a cruel business reality that Toys R Us and many other businesses learned the hard way.

Technology is fantastic, it's an essential helper of today's business. However, on its own technology will never create business value.

Creating the business value expected by your business lines demands more than deploying IT tools and infrastructure.

2. Learning from Weight Watchers and FitBit Experiences

As you've probably guessed it from the previous chapter, digital disruptions are the problem. They're kicking out of business several thousands of companies all over the world.

Disruption is one of the top buzzwords of the moment, everybody talks about it, it's used lavishly to pitch businesses, services and products.

What is it? How does it work? How to avoid it? How to take advantage of it? are the questions you may have in mind.

This chapter, based on the facts reported by Larry Dignan, ZDNet's editor-in-chief, in the very insightful, *How Apps and Wearables Upended Weight Watchers*, provides precious answers.

This chapter covers:

- What happened to Weight Watchers?
- How Fitbit disrupted the diet market?
- How digital business is changing the rules
- How the platform business model challenges today's IT

What Happened to Weight Watchers?

Let's not beat about the bush, digital disruption is what pushed Weight Watchers to the brink of bankruptcy.

Contrary to what a lot of business leaders think, digital disruption is neither a fantasy nor a buzzword.

Rather, it's a common competitive phenomenon, that's been taking out of business thousands and thousands of companies around the world.

Understanding how fitness trackers disrupted Weight Watchers, will definitely help you understand the need to urgently address the issue and properly transform with DevOps the way your company does business.

When Things Got Wrong

In 2012, the troubles Weight Watchers, the solid world leading firm in diet, faced was a bombshell. The New York based company, on the surface had a perfect business model with continuous revenue flows and large market shares.

The company suddenly faced declining subscriptions followed by dropped shares.

In a research note, now Deutsche Bank's Glen Santangelo downgraded Weight Watchers over concerns about $300 million debt payment and giving a clue to what was happening, he made it clear, "*with the proliferation of free weight loss applications (and smartphones), wearables that track fitness activity, and the combination of the two, people interested in weight loss now have more options than ever to try lose weight on their own or for free.*"

The Company's Usual Assets Got Useless

Despite its top clinically-proven weight loss programs, these brand new and free options continued to capture share of the weight loss market away from the company.

As a matter of fact, consumers were paying more attention to how many calories they burned from exercises or everyday activities. Fitness gadgets were surging in popularity with 51.2 million American adults using applications to track their health.

Wearable devices, apps, and new competitors — FitBit, Nike and JawBone — entered the weight loss and nutrition market and yanked potential customers away, they became the trend; people could lose weight on their own and for free.

In addition, other options emerged like the combination of fitness data with applications such as MyFitnessPal, and diet, made activity tracking via smartphone easier.

The Massive Effort to Stay on Top Didn't Pay Off

From a brand perspective Weight Watchers was associated with dieting and calorie counting, but not fitness.

The rescue plan set up by the management team didn't work; it was based on strong cost management, brand repositioning, product improvements, and new channel targeting in healthcare.

The aggressive steps taken to adjust marketing, continue to improve consumer offerings in both meetings and online, and right-size cost structure did not pay off.

Jim Chambers the CEO, disappointed, realized things were going bad, "*Our underlying strategies, our execution aren't what we hoped, I'm disappointed to say that we're not yet where we expected to be and that our turnaround will take longer than we had anticipated."*

Jim Chambers' effort made sense, the initiatives he took were right, the only problem was, they had nothing to do with the disruption strategies required to adjust to the expanding two-side markets.

How Fitbit Disrupted the Diet Market?

In addition to the changes in the diet market, Fitbit's irruption exacerbated the problems Weight Watchers faced.

Founded in 2007, the company sold six connected health and fitness trackers, which tracked a variety of information — users' daily steps, calories burned, distance traveled, floors climbed, and active minutes — and displayed real-time feedback to encourage customers to become more active in their daily live.

What you must definitely keep in mind is, what made these products competitive, and more importantly, disruptive is a combination of factors.

The first one is, exercise was identified as a valid alternative to dietary regimes. That changed consumers' habits.

The second is, the rise of smart devices and the associated technolgies including Internet of Things (IoT), Artificial Intelligence (AI), Big Data, and more. It opened the door to unprecedented innovation opportunities in the healthcare industry including diet.

The third and last is, the expansion of the *Network Economy* orchestrated by the increasing domination of the GAFAs' platform business model. It allows varied partnerships.

Fitbit's genius was, it took advantage of these three factors to offer innovative products, cheaper, more effective and more pleasant. They embraced the platform business model.

They anticipated customers' needs and wants as well as the breakthroughs in medical research to imagine innovative products.

They also took advantage of the platform business model to partner with some of the top technology startups to develop these innovative wearable devices and fitness trackers — Alta HR, Moov Now, Charge 3, and more.

What Fitbit did is, they disrupted the diet market.

The question you probably have in mind is, *"Platform business model, network economy, two-sided market, what's that? What's the connection with IT? What's the connection with DevOps?"* There's a connection for sure.

How Digital Business is Changing the Rules

The shift from the traditional *pipeline business model* to the *platform model* which founds the expanding digital economy which in turn is fostered and controlled by Google, Apple, Facebook, and Amazon (GAFA), is what I'd like to draw your attention to.

Misunderstanding of it, has not only led several thousands of businesses around the world to bankruptcy but also prevents IT to offer a new paradigm more focused on helping on competitiveness and revenue.

The next sections explain the differences between the two business models, their impacts on companies, and more importantly, it highlights the stakes and challenges for IT; it tells all about the digital business landscape, how it works, its structure, its players, and revenue drivers.

First, let's discuss the slowly dying pipeline business model.

The Aging Pipeline Business Model

The pipeline business model have been around since the very beginning of industries. It's widely used around the world.

It's everywhere, particularly in manufacturing; most products and services that you consume essentially comes to you through pipes.

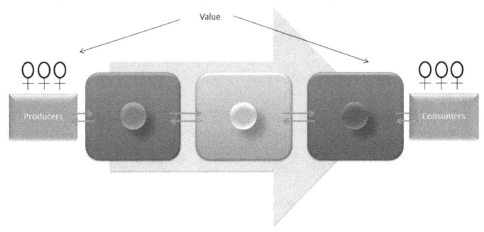

Figure 1 - The pipeline business model

As the picture illustrates, the fundamental principle is, companies create products and services, push them, and sell them across a linear value chain.

Value is produced upstream the value chain by producers and consumed downstream by consumers.

To make your understanding easy, I'll describe the pipeline model from three fundamental dimensions:

- Clients acquisition
- Innovations development
- And monetization

Let's discuss them.

Clients Are Acquired Through Lead Generation Campaigns

Acquiring clients in a pipe context is very simple. Through lead generation campaigns, potential clients — leads — are attracted in a pipeline and converted into actual customers that consume the company's products.

It's the most widespread business pattern, it's widely used in the retail industry and by online stores.

Customer Value is the Hub of Innovations Development

In the pipe context, products and services development and the associated notion of customer value are pivotal to the company's success.

Customer value refers to the money spent by the customer to buy the company's products and services; it's determined by the extent to which they meet the client expectations.

The features of the products and the services are based on the customers' needs and wants.

The one thing to keep in mind is, in the pipe thinking, as customers use products, products are valuable of themselves.

Pricing is Central in a Pipe Context

Making profit in a pipe context is based on pricing; you consider costs and augment them with your desired margin to set the price.

It's based on the notion that, customer is the only one consuming the value created by the business.

Exploring the Network Economy and the Platform Model

A platform is a business model that creates value by connecting consumers and producers.

Unlike pipelines, platforms allow their users to build their own platforms and manage their own producers and consumers.

The sum of these interconnected platforms form the hypercompetitive environments that's been kicking out of business so many companies: *The Network Economy* illustrated in figure 2.

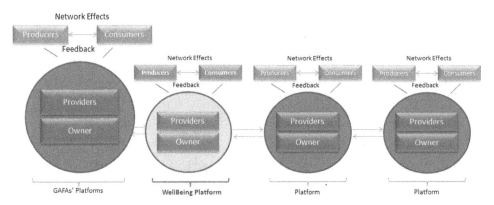

Figure 2 – The network economy resulting from expansion of the GAFAs platform model

The exhibit shows three fundamental things so many IT leaders have been ignoring or misunderstanding:

- The platform business model
- The network effects
- And the feedback

Let's explore them starting with the platform model, the network effects, and the feedback.

The Platform Business Model

The purpose of the platform model is to consummate matches among producers and consumers and to enable value creation for all users through connecting people, organizations, and resources.

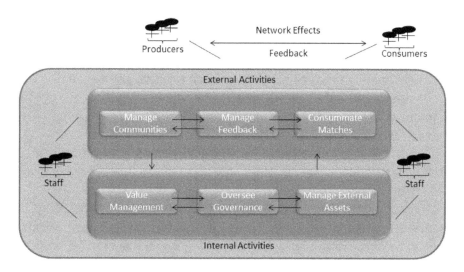

Figure 3 - General anatomy of a platform business model

In addition to the platform's owner, it involves three players including:

- The producers producing value (books and video providers)
- The consumers consuming value (those buying books and video)
- And the staff optimizing the platform

The platform provides the infrastructure, services, and the rules for the marketplace that puts together producers and consumers.

Like I did for the pipeline model, to make your understanding easy, I'll describe the platform model from three dimensions:

- Users acquisition
- Innovations development
- And monetization

Before moving forward, let's discuss the important notion of network effects and then we'll see how the platform model is revolutionizing the way we do business.

The Network Effects

Network effects refers to the impact the number of users of a platform has on the value created for each user; it's the incremental benefit gained by an existing user for each new user that joins the ecosystem.

The principle is based on the perception of both players; as more consumers join the platform, the more useful and valuable it is to producers and reversely.

The network effect is based on a variant of the supply and demand principles, *"The lower the price or the higher the quality, the higher the demand and supply and the higher the income opportunities."*

There are two types of network effects: positive and negative.

Positive network effects refers to the ability of the platform's community to produce significant value for each user of the platform. Positive feedback is key source of positive network.

A positive network effect is created for example when a Fitbit tracker is purchased without its owner intending to create value for other users, but does so regardless.

Negative network effects are those that have a negative impact compared to positive network effects. Just as positive network effects cause positive feedback loops and exponential growth, negative network effects create negative feedback and exponential decay.

The network effects are the determinant of the platform's competitiveness; it's decisive in users acquisition, innovation services development, and of course in the monetization process.

Positive Network Effects is Fundamental to Acquiring Users

To massively acquire users — producers and consumers — platform-based companies take advantage of positive network effects and feedback loops.

The idea is to build on low price or high quality products to increase consumer demands and producers offers.

Consumers' satisfaction with Fitbit trackers and their massive feedback created a positive network effects that propelled the company as the diet industry leader.

Users Concerns are the Hub of Innovations Development

Platform-based companies extensively use feedback loops to monitor customer experience and derive from them innovative service and improvement ideas.

Fitbit confirms the central role of feedback loops in improving services, *"Customer experience is really paramount to everything we do here."*

They add, *"We do a lot of customer listening. The team has a system to incorporate all of our great customer feedback into the products and services we develop."*

They argue, *"Community platforms are used "as a way to organize information around emerging issues and to troubleshoot and gather information from customers who may be experiencing a certain type of issue so that we can get a good assessment and bring that back to our engineering teams."*

Then conclude, *"Weekly reporting shares quantitative and qualitative feedback to the product and engineering teams, and the most popular ideas get integrated into future product releases."*

Monetizing

Making profit using a platform business model isn't as simple as pricing products and services and sell them to consumers. There's a charging issue, the charging opportunities vary according to businesses and industries.

When producers and consumers transact, one or both pays the platform a transaction fee.

When producers create a product or a service to engage consumers the platform may monetize consumer attention through advertising for example.

The concern underlying profitability in a platform context is, *"Who to charge for the value created."*

How Platform Models Challenge Today's IT Paradigm?

Because of the established domination of the GAFAs, the platform model is expanding and becoming a standard. It raises challenges to IT.

Meeting the Challenges of Network Effects Creation is the Bottom Line

In addition to the innovation, market responsiveness, and customer experience improvement requirements, the platform business model brings other constraints.

When you're a platform owner, you face constraints as varied as management of consumers and producers, making sure producers create value that consumers consumed, and more importantly, creating network effects.

If you're a producer, you're challenged with creating added-value products and services, and attracting and transacting with more consumers to survive and thrive.

Meeting the Challenges of Network Effects Creation Takes More than IT Tools

At this point, the question you must ask yourself is, *"Is IT's belief that cutting IT cost and speeding delivery through migrating infrastructure to the cloud is all we need to survive and thrive in the platform economy?"*

I hope you guessed it, the answer is no. Whether you're a platform owner or a producer, supplying infrastructure and delivering applications at the speed of light, on their own, will never give you the market and customer intelligence and innovation capacities needed to survive and thrive in the platform economy.

What You Must Keep in Mind

The diet industry's disruption fostered by the irruption of wearable devices, Internet of Things (IoT), and Artificial Intelligence (AI) technologies led Weight Watchers on the verge of bankruptcy.

People at Fitbit never thought that migrating infrastructure to the cloud and automating IT operations were enough.

Rather, they paid attention to the changes in the diet industry — incumbents' strengths and weaknesses, consumers expectations, product substitution opportunities — and through varied partnerships with platform owners and producers set up their own platform to disrupt Weight Watchers.

Let me say that again, technology is fantastic, it's an essential helper of today's business. However, on its own it'll never generate revenue and make the business competitive; it demands more than deploying IT tools.

3. Why Today's DevOps Practices Can't Meet the Challenges

Despite the massive buzzword, the business value of DevOps — yet presented as the solution to all business problems — is increasingly questioned.

The truth no one wants to talk about is, several factors prevent the adoption of DevOps as a business solution.

These factors include:

- The fact that, its business principles and benefits which apply well beyond software concerns are ignored by the IT community
- The unfortunate fact that, IT vendors use the word DevOps as a marketing argument to sell automation tools
- And the never mentioned fact that, people understand DevOps culture in theory and struggle to implement it as a tangible business capability

This chapter clarifies the following issues:

- DevOps is underexploited
- The irrelevant IT's tool-centered perspective
- DevOps is primarily a business culture

DevOps is Underexploited

One thing confusing with today's DevOps approach is, the features likely to help the company survive the digital competition and thrive, are totally ignored by IT practitioners.

The fact of the matter is, DevOps is underexploited. The Agile, Lean, and innovation aspects of it are drowned in massive marketing campaigns suggesting that the so-called DevOps tools are what matter.

The non-technological features of DevOps are either rejected or underestimated by the vast majority of IT experts; they refuse to see the evidence that the competitive advantages needed to meet the disrupted market challenges expected from DevOps result from their adoption across the organization.

CA Technologies DevOps Strategist Brad Wolfe confirms that point in a comment on LinkedIn, "*It's a message many don't want to hear but must acknowledge to be successful.*"

Agile practices by speeding up work flows, problem solving, and decision-making and establishing cross-functional collaboration, not only make the business responsive to market opportunities but also create flexible work environments that are conducive to innovation.

You'll never achieve that with IT tools alone!

Similarly, Lean practices by spreading across the organization the importance of continuously optimizing processes, improving product and service quality, and stressing customer benefits, institutionalize a culture of value.

Once again, technology alone isn't enough to help you.

Do you honestly believe that, to compete with the GAFAs and thrive in the highly competitive network economy, the only thing would be to deploy Github, Jenkins, Chef, Docker, Microservices, and wait that benefits happen?

I hope you don't!

Let's leave it aside, just keep in mind at this poin that, the organizational infrastructure — staff, interactions, value, practices — of DevOps is where business benefits and competitiveness are created.

The IT's Tool-Centered Perspective is Now Irrelevant

IT vendors, their consultants, and the CIOs they convinced, do not hesitate to promote the business value DevOps tools alone can bring.

Regardless of whether you adopted a pipeline business model or a platform model, these statements are false, they're totally disconnected from the way business benefits is created.

In a pipeline context, business value clearly relates to the revenue generated from the money spent by customers to buy your company's products and services.

In a two-side market context, revenue results from a combination of factors including network effects, market visibility, inbound marketing effectiveness, innovation capacity, organizational agility, operational responsiveness, and strongly engaged community. This is how business value is created.

That's what famous strategic management gurus like Michael Porter, Henry Mintzberg, Sangeet Paul Choudary, and Geoffrey G. Parker and late Peter Drucker and Michael Hammer, have been teaching top business leaders around the globe.

The questions that are increasingly asked are, *"Where did DevOps vendors and experts get the idea that GitHub, Jenkins, Chef, and Docker on their own can create business value?"* *" What are their motives?"* And more importantly, *"How come several hundreds thousands IT leaders around the world keep buying the promise that GitHub, Jenkins, Chef, and Docker on their own will generate the expected business benefits?"*

Moreover, lines of business' bottom line isn't the deployment of DevOps tools neither the extensive automation of IT operations.

It's the transformation of the business required to help them survive and thrive in markets dominated by the GAFA.

As seen in chapters one and two, the stake for your lines of business is to survive the irruption of the GAFA in their industry and the expansion of the network economy by establishing the conditions to making the business agile, responsive to markets, and more importantly, make them top innovative disruptors.

DevOps is a Software Deployment Culture Thought for Business Performance

Being the disruptor and not the disrupted is the competitive attitude businesses must embrace if they want to meet the challenges of their disrupted markets and make profit.

Adopting DevOps culture is likely to help them meet these challenges.

Shared across the organization, it creates the conditions for agility, collaboration, responsiveness, visibility, and innovation.

Before moving forward, let's get a clear understanding of what culture is and how it applies to business.

A great definition is given by late Leopold Sedar Senghor, a Senegalese politician, poet, and cultural theorist who defined it as, *" The set of beliefs, values, habits, behaviors, practices, and tools a specific human community shares to survive a specific environment."*

Figure 4 - DevOps Culture Illustrated

As the picture illustrates, the DevOps culture is the set of values, habits, behaviors, practices, and tools the organization's staff share to make the business a market disruptor and profitable.

What's not being said is, implementing DevOps is primarily about getting the organization's staff agree upon and adopt the six elements likely to make the business competitive, profitable and market disruptor:

People – DevOps is a human problem. People are pivotal to the creation of the expected business value.

People have the imagination and the creativity underpinning innovation; they're the one creating and nurturing the dynamics that makes the company competitive and profitable.

Values – Values are the key determinant of the business competitiveness and profitability. They are beliefs doubled with behaviors whose objective is to keep people focused on the factors identified as likely to make the business a market disruptor.

The DevOps values that I recommend to my clients include:

- Collaborative mindset
- Customer satisfaction
- Customer experience continuous improvement
- Practice continuous improvement
- Revenue continuous generation

Behavior – It's an essential determinant of the business competitiveness and value creation. When the staff behavior doesn't reflect the values shared across the business, the company as a human organization dismantles, loses market shares and goes bankrupt.

The behaviors that I recommend to my clients include:

- Favor collaborative work over anything else
- Accelerate problem solving and decision-making
- Commit to the company's values, objectives, services, and customers

Practices – Are the carefully selected activities performed by the staff in an effort to make the company competitive and generate the expected business benefits.

The practices I recommend to my clients are a collection of well selected best practices in the areas of:

- Disruptive Innovation Management (DIM)
- Customer Relationships Management (CRM)
- Agile software development
- IT operations management

Tools – Tools as the name suggests are the IT tools the staff, across the organization use to make the business competitive and profitable.

My recommendations aren't restricted to the usual DevOps tools, they embrace areas unexplored by today's DevOps practices including:

- Market research
- Disruptive innovation management
- Customer Relationship Management (CRM)
- And of course automation tools

The key thing to keep in mind about DevOps culture is, culture is a fantastic means to get the business strategy executed; by engraving in people mind the performance key drivers—People, value, behavior, practices, tools—they instinctively act in line with the company's core interests.

What You Must Keep in Mind

As I attempted to demonstrate it in this chapter, DevOps is great but several gray areas remain about how to implement it as the catalyst of the business competitiveness.

Today's DevOps practices focused on software deployment and IT operations do not deliver the expected business benefits, I'm talking about business benefits.

As long as DevOps implementations do not result in business capabilities that help companies meet their disrupted market challenges, claiming any business value is misleading business leaders.

Implementing DevOps culture into a business capability that makes the company a competitive and profitable top disruptor is the topic of the next chapter.

4. Implementing DevOps Culture As Business Capabilities

DevOps is implemented today's as an IT capability that yield very few business benefits. A DevOps implementation look more like an IT modernization initiative than a business growth and competitiveness strategy.

The reason so many of them fail to deliver the expected business benefits is, the vast majority of experts not only lack understanding of the digital business environment, but more importantly, they lack the basic business transformation skills.

They struggle to translate the notion of DevOps culture into competitive and profitable business capabilities.

The key to unlock the business benefits of DevOps is your ability to translate its culture into a business capability.

This chapter covers:

- DevOps implementation's stakes and challenges
- DevOps founding fathers' vision and approach
- How to translating DevOps culture into a business capability

DevOps Implementation's Stakes and Challenges

The problem is, today's DevOps practices aren't tailored to address the required transformations; they're focused on applications development and deployment and are narrowed to continuous delivery infrastructure.

Increasingly, surveys, case studies, and testimonies bring out the gaps between the business expectations and DevOps implementations.

Delivering more software, cheaper, and faster isn't enough to make a business competitive and profitable.

They Sell IT Transformation as DevOps Implementation, Don't Be Fooled, Don't Buy It

Imagine you're a business and you want to transform your travel agency business to anticipate Amazon's irruption in the industry.

You heard about the power of DevOps, you hire a consulting company (one of the big four), and beg them to help you, *"To survive and thrive, we need to get a capability that increases our capacity to deliver innovations cheaper and faster."*

If at the presentation meeting, you see lots of architecture schemes explaining, *"How GitHub, Jenkins, Docker, Chef, and more will foster innovation, establish collaboration, bring in revenue,"* be careful; chances are they're trying to transform your IT and sell it to you as a typical DevOps transformation.

Don't buy it, run away!

IT transformation is neither the stake nor the challenge, transforming the business through adjusting it to the requirements of your disrupted markets is what you should focus on.

Adjusting to Disrupted Markets is the Ignored and Unprecedented Stake

Most DevOps implementation initiatives are disconnected from any business concern; they're conducted as if, deploying the so called DevOps tools was enough to make the business competitive.

Let's face it, the challenge for business lines is to transform so that they survive and thrive in the competitive environment imposed by the GAFAs: the *Network Economy.*

The bottom line is to properly answer three fundamental questions:
1. Which one of the pipeline or platform business model best fits your business?
2. How to change your structure, staff and skills, processes and practices, tools and infrastructure, values and beliefs to optimize either your pipeline model or implement a platform model?
3. How to get these changes implemented and adopted across your organization?

As you can see from these three questions, pretending that migrating infrastructure to the cloud or deploying GitHub, Jenkins, Docker, and Chef is enough to make the business competitive is a joke, a big one.

Nine West Holdings, The Bon-Ton Stores, Toys R Us, Remington, Southeastern Grocers, Tops Markets, and recently Sears; learned it the hard way, *business transformation was the way to go.*

Adopting the recent IT innovations to meet the challenges of the rising digital business isnt't only a matter of changing the technology but primarily a business transformation affair.

The question you might have in mind right now is, *"Ok, I got it, now, how to implement DevOps in a way that boosts our competitiveness?"*

Translating DevOps Culture into a Capability is the Unknown Challenge

Contrary to what you've read in magazines and blog posts, or heard in webinars, conferences, DevOps is not a continuous delivery infrastructure (CDI).

Don't Be Fooled by Misleading Marketing

Don't be fooled by the massive marketing out there, its primary purpose is to sell you tools, platforms and infrastructure.

If your concern is accelerating application development and deployment, don't waste time and money with DevOps, deploying Agile will be cheaper and suited for you goals.

If your concern is optimizing IT operations, again, don't waste time and money, invest either in ITIL or in CDI.

On the other hand, if you want to modernize your IT so that it plays a role in your company's competitiveness, implementing DevOps into a business capability is the recommended option.

Translating Culture into Capabilities is the Challenge

Make no mistake about it, to make DevOps the foundation of your competitiveness, you'll have to convert its culture into a business capability.

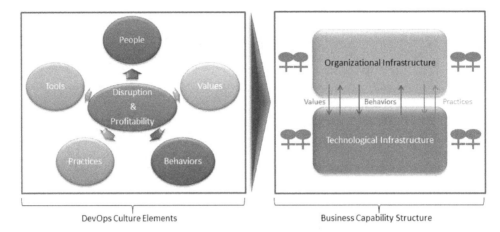

Figure 5 - From DevOps culture to business capability

DevOps is primarily a software deployment culture tailored for innovation, competitiveness, and revenue. That's what I got from my experience deploying it to help companies boost their business.

As illustrated, the challenge is to translate the elements of the DevOps culture — people, values, behaviors, practices and tools — into a tangible business capability including an organizational infrastructure and a technological infrastructure.

Organizational infrastructure refers to the non-technological aspects of the business including structure, staff and skills, processes and practices, and values and beliefs.

Technological infrastructure as the name suggests is the set of tools, technologies, and infrastructure the company mobilizes to support its organizational infrastructure.

DevOps Founding Fathers' Vision and Approach

Before moving forward with the DevOps culture implementation process, I'd like to share with you the vision and approach of its founding fathers including Patrick Debois, John Allspaw, Jez Humble, and Gene Kim.

Although the vast majority reduce it to the means to deliver more software, cheaper, and faster, some define it beyond software deployment concerns and see it primarily as a system of people and skills, processes and practices, values and behaviors, and automation tools, specifically put together to make the business competitive. They're right.

One of them is Adam Jacob, co-founder and CTO of Chef. Here is what he says in a remarkable article: *The Secret of DevOps, It's Always Been About People, Not Technology.*

The Foundational Article: The Secret of DevOps, It's Always Been About People, Not Technology

A careful analysis of what Jacob says shows that, unlike the overwhelming majority of practitioners, he sees DevOps as a two-building blocks capability including something that looks like an organizational infrastructure and a technological infrastructure.

DevOps Does Have an Organizational Infrastructure

Here is what he says about the non-technological aspects of DevOps, « *DevOps is fundamentally about taking the behaviors and beliefs that draw us together as people, combining them with a deep understanding of our customers' needs, and using that knowledge to ship better products to our customers.* »

The Technological Infrastructure is Essential

But he makes it clear, "*Tools matter. Make no mistake, trying to change the way you work without changing the mechanisms by which you do that work is a futile exercise in excruciating failure. But tools exist in service of the prime directive: building highly functioning, highly effective cross-functional teams, that attack your thorniest business problems as a unit, rather than as lone individuals or silos with competing incentives.*»

Modeling DevOps Founding Fathers' Vision into a Business Capability

Modeling Jacob's perspective gives the following capability architecture:

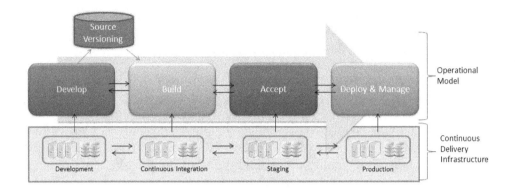

Figure 6 - DevOps business capability

Unlike today's DevOps practices which stress the CDI, DevOps is made up of two primary components:

- The ignored business operational model
- The well-known continuous delivery infrastructure

Let's discuss them!

The Operational Model is Where Value is Created

Many IT practitioners ignore it, the operational model is where the expected business benefits are created. It's actually the *value chain* of your organization's, it's the set of interactions, staff and skills, processes and practices, values and behaviors, and tools and infrastructure mobilized across the organization to repeatedly generate business benefits.

A business benefit is either the revenue generated from the money spent by customers to buy the company's products or anything likely to turn into a revenue. A customer's expense with the company, market share, rapid time-to-revenue, accelerated time-to-market, and high ROI are examples of business value.

On the other hand, system availability, network, storage, server, and application capacities aren't business benefits, they're IT benefits.

Business value is created as part of a cross-functional process that cuts across the entire operational model from the *Plan & Measure* and *Develop & Test* to *Release & Deploy* and *Monitor & Improve*.

It starts with spotting customer needs and wants, moves forward with translating needs and wants into innovate service ideas, then moves on with developing the service ideas into tangible innovative services, and ends with rolling out the services and continuously improving customer experience.

As you can see, optimizing your operational model is the surest way to guarantee business value, not only IT implementation.

The CDI is Wrongly Referred to as DevOps

As we've seen in the previous section, seeking to create business value with DevOps by narrowing it to a CDI doesn't make sense. The CDI is structured into a set of technical environments providing infrastructure and tools supporting each step of the operational model. They include:

- Develop – Platform providing software development and unit testing environment and associated tools.
- Continuous Integration (CI) – Platform providing software integration and testing environment and associated tools
- Staging – Platform supporting acceptance tests including User Acceptance Test (UAT) and Operational Acceptance Test (OAT)

To win in today's disrupted markets, businesses need to establish innovation culture, develop revenue-oriented mindset, become responsive to market opportunities. It takes more than just deploying Git, Jenkins, Chef, Puppet, and Docker onto the CDI.

These fantastic tools will optimize and accelerate applications delivery processes. Unfortunately, unless the operational model is optimized, on their own, they will never, on their own, deliver the expected business benefits.

Converting DevOps Culture a Business Capability

The bottom line is to implement the two-building block capability as your company's value chain and then make sure the interactions are optimized and the shared values, behaviors, and practices are widely adopted to make the business competitive.

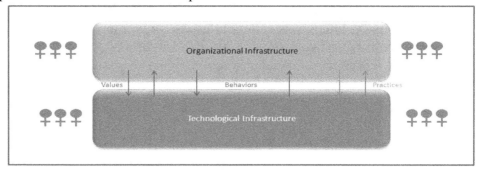

Figure 7 - Two-building block business capability

The DevOps culture translation into a business capability is two-fold including the implementation of the organizational structure and the deployment of the technological infrastructure.

Let's discuss them !

Translating the Organizational Aspects of DevOps Culture

The objective here is to choose the right business model — pipeline or platform — for your company, assess the impacts and define the changes before deploy it across your company's value chain.

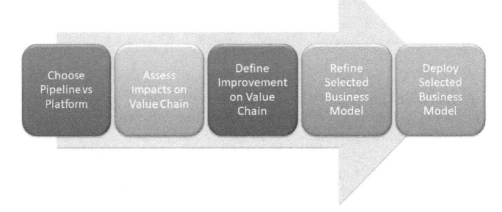

Figure 8 - Translating organizational features into capability

The above five-step framework facilitates and accelerates the organizational infrastructure design and deployment.

Let's discuss its steps!!

Choosing between Pipeline and Platform Business Models

The bottom line in this step is to assess your competitive environment and choose between the pipeline or the platform business model?

The following questionnaire summarizes the key issues to address:

Questions	Answers
Spot the changes in your disrupting / disrupted market?	
Identify your market disruption drivers?	
Is the pipeline model the best option for your business? Why?	
Is the platform model the best option for your business? Why?	
Discuss the selected model at the executive level	

Assessing the Impacts on the Current Value Chain

This step is about identifying and assessing the impacts of the selected business model on your current value chain. The following questionnaire summarizes the key issues to address:

Questions	Answers
How does the selected model – pipeline or platform–affect the interactions within your value chain?	
Same question about your staff and sills	
Same question about your values and beliefs	
Same question about your processes and practices	
Same question about your tools, technologies, and infrastructure	

Defining the Improvements on the Current Value Chain

In this step the challenge is to identify the improvements and changes to make to your current value chain. The following questionnaire summarizes the key issues to address:

Questions	Answers
What are the gaps between the current value chain and the selected business model---pipeline or platform?	
What are the potential improvements for the partnership perspective?	
What are the improvements from the staff and skills standpoint?	
What are the improvements from processes and practices perspective?	
What are the potential improvements from the values and beliefs perspective?	

Refining the Selected Business Model

This step is about redesigning the current value chain based on the selected business model. The following questionnaire summarizes the key issues to address:

Questions	Answers
Are their specific features of the selected business model that need customization?	
Are there features to customize from the partnership perspective?	
Are there features to customize from the staff and skills perspective?	
Are there specific features to customize from the processes and practices perspective?	
Are there specific features to customize from the values and beliefs perspective?	

Deploying the Selected Business Model

This step is about deploying your future pipeline-based or platform-based business model across your organization. Executing information and training campaigns aiming at accelerating the adoption of changes is the focus.

The following questionnaire summarizes the key issues to address:

Questions	Answers
Will you need a pilot experiment project before deploying the organizational infrastructure across your company?	
Will you need a roadmap supporting the organizational infrastructure deployment?	
What are the key messages of your information campaign?	
What are the key training of your training campaign?	
What staff is concerned with the training campaign?	
What entity should play the DevOps culture custodian? The PMO? Other?	

Translating the Technological Features of DevOps Culture

The bottom line here is to define continuous delivery policy to apply to your organization and derive from it the cloud architecture that will host your continuous delivery infrastructure.

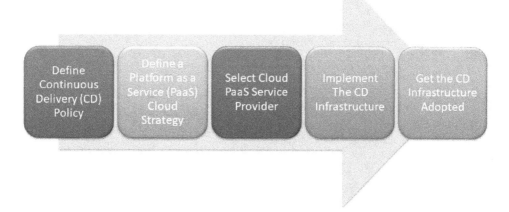

Figure 9 - Translating technological features into capability

The above five-step framework facilitates and accelerates the design and implementation of your next technological infrastructure.

Let's discuss it!

Defining Continuous Delivery (CD) Policy

The bottom line here is to define your company's next CD policy. The following questionnaire summarizes the key issues to address:

Questions	Answers
Why Continuous Integration (CI) would (or wouldn't) be the best fit for your deployment policy?	
Why Continuous Delivery would (or wouldn't) be the best fit for your deployment policy?	
Why Continuous Deployment would (or wouldn't) be the best fit for your deployment policy?	

Defining PaaS Cloud Strategy

The objective in this step is to clarify your Platform-as-a-Service (PaaS) cloud strategy along with the architecture that will host your CDI.

The following questionnaire summarizes the key issues to address:

Questions	Answers
What option is best for your PaaS cloud? Public? Private? Hybrid?	
Why public PaaS cloud would be the best option for your technological infrastructure?	
Why private PaaS cloud would be the best option for your technological infrastructure?	
Why hybrid PaaS cloud would be the best option for your technological infrastructure?	
Are you considering managed or co-located hosting?	

Selecting PaaS Cloud Service Provider

Selecting your PaaS cloud service provider and defining SLA intended to support the partnership is the objective here.

The following questionnaire summarizes the key issues to address:

Questions	Answers
Why would (or wouldn't) you consider Amazon AWS?	
Why would (or wouldn't) you consider Microsoft Azure?	
Why would (or wouldn't) you consider Google Cloud?	
Why would (or wouldn't) you consider Rackspace?	
Why would (or wouldn't) you consider other cloud service providers?	

Implementing the CD Infrastructure

The bottom line here is the implementation and deployment of the CD infrastrure. The following questionnaire summarizes the key issues to address:

Questions	Answers
Why would (or wouldn't) you hire a consulting for implementation?	
Why would (or wouldn't) you consider in-house implementation?	

Getting the CD Infrastructure Adopted

The objectif in this final step is to execute the information and training campaigns aiming at accelerating the adoption of the CDI.

The following questionnaire summarizes the key issues to address:

Questions	Answers
Will you need a pilot experiment project before deploying the technological infrastructure across your company?	
Will you need a roadmap supporting the technological infrastructure deployment?	
What are the key messages of your information campaign?	
What are the key training of your training campaign?	
What staff is concerned with the training campaign?	

What You Must Keep in Mind

Never lose sight of that, DevOps is not the toolchain certain IT vendors and unfortunately CIOs have been wrongly selling to business lines as the capability that'll make them competitive.

DevOps is a software deployment culture that seeks to make the business innovative, responsive, and profitable; it's likely to change not only the way you do IT, but more importantly, the way your company does business.

DevOps culture is a powerful abstract concept that translates in the form of a two-component business capability including the organizational infrastructure and the technological infrastructure.

DevOps' organizational infrastructure is the most important, the most strategic piece of it, it's where the expected business revenue and competitive advantages are created.

5. How DevOps Enables Platform Model: The WellBeing Case

Many companies are reluctant to invest in DevOps because they struggle to picture the way it works in daily business.

The concerns are many:

- How does it concretely work on the ground?
- What are the daily activities? How does it concretely materialize?
- How are the roles and responsibilities shared in the organization?
- What are the major interactions? Who are the players?

These are only some the questions I've been facing in all the conferences I give around the world.

In order to concretely answer about the daily functioning of DevOps, I'll tell you how a major player in the diet and healthcare markets, I had the honor to advise few months ago, has been using it as the foundation of its digital business.

This case study will give you an overview of how WellBeing, the fictitious name of a real company, uses DevOps to thrive in the Network Economy.

This chapter covers:

- WellBeing Corporation – market, product and mission
- How DevOps enabled WellBeing platform model
- DevOps' daily operations at WellBeing

WellBeing Corporation – Market, Product, and Mission

WellBeing Inc is an American company headquartered in San Francisco, California. It was founded in 2010 by three business development consultants who struggled to give a fresh start to their career.

Adopting the Platform Strategy to Lead the Diet Industry and Thrive in the Network Economy

The company is immersed in and leads the diet industry and leverages the platform business model to offer activity trackers and wireless-enabled wearable technology devices.

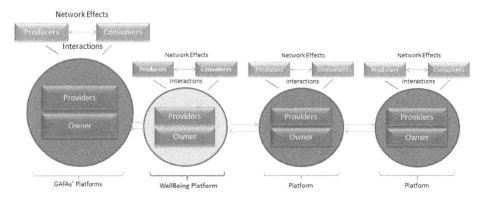

Figure 10 - WellBeing's competitive context

WellBeing's seeks to empower and inspire its customers to live healthier and more active lives.

To achieve that mission, the company builds on a platform business model and enjoys several business benefits:

- WellBeing's Platform which automates and enables the company's activity
- Google Cloud Platform (GCP) which allows the company to cut operational costs and drive down prices to create positive network effects
- A very active community of millions of users providing feedback that contribute to improving the company's products
- High return partnerships with producers particularly third-party developers who provide APIs to connect to the platform or create health and fitness mobile apps

Navigating WellBeing's Platform Business Model

The genius of WellBeing's founders is, unlike its competitors, they reinvented the company's business model, that is to say the way they work.

Figure 11 gives an overview of WellBeing DevOps-based platform business model:

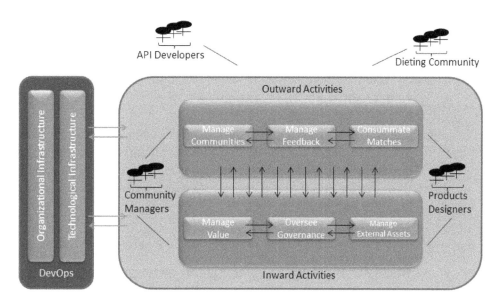

Figure 11 - WellBeing's platform business model

The figure highlights four key elements of business growth and performance including:

- User community and the network effects it creates
- Business activities geared towards outside
- Inward-looking business activities
- DevOps' influence

Let's discuss them.

The **User Community** consists of two types of actors whose role is to create positive network effects in an effort to continuously generate value for the platform: APIs developers and the dieting community.

APIs Developers' role is to create health and fitness apps as well as APIs that continuously attract additional developers.

Dieting Community, by using wearable devices and fitness trackers, and by providing feedback contribute to the platform monetization.

Outward and inward activities act like feedback loops in an effort to keep network effects positive.

Outward activities are performed by community management teams to monitor the external business environment.

In addition, their purpose ist to not only make sure customer experience is continuously positive but also that APIs developers benefit the best conditions to continuously contribute to the company's positive network effects.

Inward activities are performed by the company's staff, particularly community managers and products designers.

Their purpose is to monitor created value, make decision on how to increase it, monitor the changes in the ecosystem, make decision on how to take advantage of them, and design new products or improve existing products.

In addition to acting as an orchestrator and coordinator of WellBeing's added-value activities, DevOps through its organizational infrastructure not only changes the company's way of doing business but also creates the conditions for operational agility and flexibility, customer experience focus, and collaborative mindset.

How DevOps Enables WellBeing's Platform Model

As figure 12 illustrates it, in addition to orchestrating and coordinating WellBeing's outward and inward activities, DevOps acts as an enabler of the company's digital strategy.

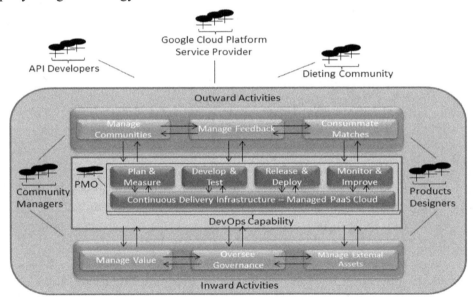

Figure 12 - DevOps-enabled platform business model

Two elements play a pivotal role, they include:

- The two-component DevOps capability which is the operational translation of DevOps culture
- The Project Management Office (PMO) which acts as the custodian of the DevOps culture

Let's discuss them.

How DevOps Enables the Platform Model's Values

The objective of the company's digital strategy is to continuously matches demand from both sides – API developers and dieting community – and keep network effects positive.

The platform takes advantage of three levers enabled by DevOps to achieve the objective, they include:

- The quality of the infrastructure provided to the APIs Developers
- The innovative activity trackers
- Activity trackers affordability

How DevOps Makes Quality Infrastructure a Competitive Advantage

Providing premium experience to APIs developers through high quality development infrastructure is one of their top competitive advantage.

What happens is, developers enjoy developing APIs not only for platforms that have massive players but also for those that make their job easier.

The Google Application Engine (GAE) platform supporting WellBeing's continuous delivery infrastructure, is made available to API developers and businesses; it allows them to build and run applications using Google's advanced infrastructure.

How DevOps Makes Activity Trackers a Competitive Advantage

Making activity trackers affordable to create positive network effects is another top competitive advantage.

WellBeing builds on the proven principle of *demand side economies of scale* that, the value of a product or service increases in accordance with the number of users of that product or service.

Taking advantage of a managed PaaS cloud platform, allows the company to get rid of the hassle of managing IT, and more importantly, of substantial infrastructure and operational costs.

The resulting saving makes it possible to lower prices and create powerful network effects.

How DevOps Makes Innovation a WellBeing's Competitive Advantage

Continuously improving activity trackers with innovations to create network effects is the company's top competitive advantages.

The company builds on the belief that, innovation is more successful when there is a critical mass or network effect in an industry or market.

Deploying and getting adopted DevOps' organizational infrastructure resulted in the institutionalization of Agile and Lean practices as well as the establishment of collaboration, innovation, and customer satisfaction mindsets.

They were conducive to powerful network effects creation.

The Agile PMO as DevOps Culture Custodian

The challenge as identified by the WellBeing's executive team was to make sure, true DevOps culture is applied. The bottom line was to take advantage of mechanisms that guarantee adequate application of DevOps principles.

The company made the choice to use the Agile PMO as custodian of the DevOps culture. It assists and facilitates the following issues:

- Tracking changes in the external business environments and assessing the impacts on network effects
- Prioritizing, setting up and overseeing project portfolios focused on network effects issues
- Assessing and improving DevOps culture influence on the company's network effects
- Evangelizing on DevOps culture particularly on how it helps to improve positive network effects

DevOps' Daily Operations at WellBeing

The DevOps capability that resulted from the implementation of DevOps culture acts like a state machine; it's based on a feedback loop that helps to monitor the company's network effects and decide on the actions to take.

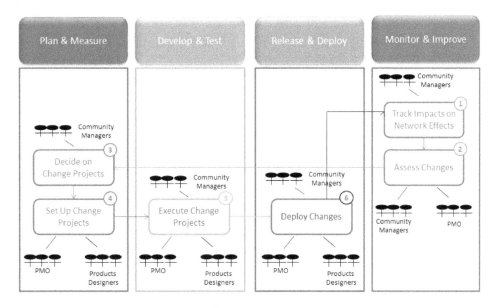

Figure 13 - DevOps daily operations at WellBeing

WellBeing's DevOps activities are structured around a four-stage lifecycle that orchestrates the execution of the company's digital strategy.

Each stage involves specific staff and skills and mobilizes adequate methodologies and tools. Let's take a look at how it works.

Monitoring and Improve

WellBeing uses that stage as the starting point of the feedback loop supporting its digital strategy execution.

Tracking Impacts on the Network Effects

This task tracks the changes in the external business environment and the impacts on the company's network effects.

Several staff track on a daily basis the external and internal business environments to anticipate potential impacts on the company's network effects.

They include:

- Community managers who act as product owners to analyze CRM system information to see what can be learned about APIs developers and dieting community experience
- IT operations and Google Cloud support who act as contributors by providing and analyzing system logs to see what can be learned from them

- The PMO who makes sure the principles of DevOps organizational infrastructure are properly applied

Assess Impacts on the Network Effects

The purpose of this activity is to assess the impacts on WellBeing's network effects and identify improvements.

The same staff are mobilized to assess the impacts on the company's network effects, their respective duties include:

- Community managers who check the likeliness of product prices and usage as well as infrastructure quality to positively impact the company's network effects
- IT operations and Rackspace staff who audit system settings to make sure the infrastructure quality positively impacts the network effects
- The PMO who audits how well are used the principles of DevOps' organizational infrastructure and the resulting impacts on the network effects

Plan and Measure

The stake at this stage is to identify, set up, and kick off the change projects likely to keep effective the company's network effects.

Decide on Change Projects

The bottom line here is to identify and define the change projects which are likely to keep effective WellBeing's network effects.

Several competencies are involved in this task, they include:

- Community managers who leverage business requirements lists (Product Backlog is scrum agile terminology) and project prioritization lists (Sprint Backlog in scrum agile terminoly) to identify and prioritize change projects
- IT operations and Google Cloud support who act as contributors to confirm or infirm feasibility
- The PMO who makes sure the principles of DevOps organizational infrastructure, particularly agile project management practices are properly applied

Set Up Change Projects

The objective in this stage is to assign the human and financial resources as well as the DevOps assistant to the selected change projects.

The Agile PMO leads this task assisted by relevant staff; he collaborates with the product design and community manager teams to identify and assign relevant external and internal stakeholders.

Additional tasks including agreement on budget, timeline and key success factors.

Develop and Test

The objective in this step is to execute the change projects identified as business priorities. It's focused on executing the selected change projects.

It includes the following activities:

- Innovation, functional and technical requirements capture
- Activity tracker's software and hardware development
- Activity tracker's software and hardware testing

Several competencies are involved in this task, they include:

- Product designers who leverage varied software and hardware methodologies and tools — UML, Microservices, Scrum agile, X programming (XP), Design Thinking — to upgrade existing activity trackers or develop new ones
- Community managers, IT operations and Rackspace support staff who contribute to the development and unit testing as needed
- The PMO who makes sure the principles of DevOps organizational infrastructure, particularly agile software development practices are properly applied

Release and Deploy

The purpose of this stage is to ensure a continuous delivery of the innovative updates and new activity trackers' features resulting from the execution of the change projects.

Product designers, community managers, IT operations and the PMO are involved in this task.

It builds on GAE's deployment pipeline and is primarily driven by the product designer teams.

What You Must Keep in Mind

The WellBeing case tells four unprecedented lessons on DevOps implementation, and more importantly, on business transformation:

- DevOps isn't the end but the means to achieve business goals: creating powerful network effects
- To disrupt the diet market and challenge Weight Watchers, WellBeing adopted the platform business model
- To take advantage of the benefits of the platform model, particularly network effects creation, WellBeing transformed the way it works and does business
- The organizational and technological infrastructures of DevOps are the key to unlocking the drivers of network effects

Unlike many of your IT peers, never forget that the primary goal of IT, therefore DevOps, is to concretely enable business benefits. Implementing DevOps for the sake of implementing it doesn't make sense.

Many made expensive investments in DevOps, thinking business benefits will be miraculously generated. They were wrong, DevOps delivers the expected business benefits when it's used as the means to achieve your business strategy.

Many are denying the digital disruption reality, they wrongly think it's a marketing invention to make the buzz and then money.

Digital disruption has been kicking out of business companies that deny it, refuse to transform, and unproperly transformed.

As we'll see in the next chapter digital transformation isn't narrowed to migrating IT infrastructure to cloud and implementing continuous delivery infrastructure (CDI), containers, Big Data, Artificial Intelligence (AI).

It's primarily about making your company's value chain agile, flexible, and responsive in a way that makes it conducive to network effects creation.

6. Business Architecture for Successful Digital Organizations

At this point, you're probably saying, *"Okay I got it, the GAFAs have created new and hypercompetitive two-side markets where technology's productivity alone isn't enough to survive and thrive. Being innovative, responsive, agile, and flexible is urgent."*

You're probably thinking, *"It's true that there's a non-technological dimension for getting these competitive edges and if the DevOps organizational infrastructure allows to get them, so yes DevOps is the solution."*

And then finally you might be wondering, *"What does the digital organization look like? What's its structure? How does it work? Is there any applicable framework?"*

This chapter provides guidance on transforming businesses to digital relying on DevOps.

This chapter answers these fundamental questions, it covers:

- The three dimensions of successful digital organizations
- The pipeline-based digital organization
- The platform-based digital organization

Three Dimensions of Successful Digital Organizations

The digital organization is the basic model of structure, staff, skills, processes, practices, values, behaviors, tools and infrastructure your company needs to succeed in today's disrupted markets.

It answers the question many have been asking, *"What should we do to prosper in markets disrupted by Google, Amazon, Facebook, Apple, and Walmart?"*

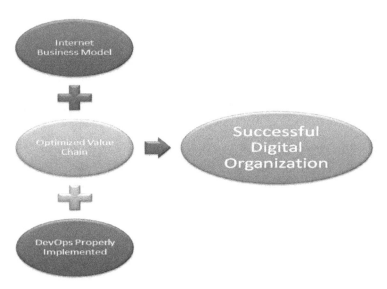

Figure 14 - The simple equation of successful digital organization

As figure 14 illustrates, three elements determine successful digital businesses, they include:

- Adoption of the internet business model
- Value chain optimization
- And proper DevOps implementation

Let's discuss the reasons they're the key determinants of any successful digital organization.

Adopting the Internet Business Model

As surprising as it may sound, many IT leaders misunderstand business models, they confuse it with the revenue model.

That's one of the reasons most IT transformations result in no tangible business benefits.

A revenue model is a framework for generating revenues; it identifies the revenue sources to pursue, the value to offer, pricing, and who to charge.

However, revenue model is part of the company's business model. Clarifying them is useful.

The business model describes the principles, philosophy, and practices underpinning the way a business generates value.

It's the very specific set of added-value staff and skills, values and beliefs, processes and practices, and tools and infrastructure mobilized by the organization to generate value.

It's worth reiterating it, the purpose of IT is to enable the business model and, it'll never achieve that without any understanding of business models.

As you got it from the traditional business model definition, internet business models refer to the principles, philosophy, and practices underpinning the way the business makes money on the internet.

The pipeline and platform business models discussed in the previous chapters, are internet business models that help companies survive the domination of the GAFAs and thrive.

Optimizing the Organization's Value Chain

The value chain is concept developed by strategy Professor Michael Porter of the University of Hardvard.

Understanding Michael Porter's Value Chain

It's the idea that, to generate profit, the company relies on two categories of very specific added-value activities: support and primary.

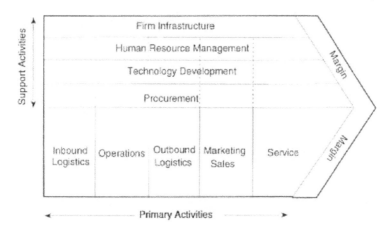

Figure 15 - Original value chain model

The primary activities are directly involved in the value creation process, they include:

- *Inbound Logistics* which refers to the supply chain processes, they're about receiving, storing, and distributing raw materials needed to manufacture products.
- *Operations* which refers to the transformation processes, they're about transforming raw materials into products and services sold to customers.

- *Outbound Logistics* which refers to the distribution processes, they're about delivering products and services to customers.
- *Marketing and Sales*, as the name suggests, refers to the processes leveraged to persuade clients to purchase the company's products and services.
- *Service* refers to post sales activities, they're about maintaining the value of the products and services to the customers, once it's been purchased.

The support activities also called indirect processes include:
- *Firm Infrastructure* which refers to the company's systems and functions supporting the daily operations.
- *Human Resource (HR) Management* which relates to the recruiting, hiring, training, rewarding and retaining processes of the organization.
- *Procurement* which refers to the purchase and vendor management processes of the organization.
- *Technology*, these processes relate to managing and processing information as well as protecting the organization's expertise.

The Fundamental Reason Why Understanding the Value Chain Matters

Some people often ask me, " *Why do you stress so much the value chain? Many companies make money without it.* "

My answer is always the same, " *Whether or not you're aware of it, there is a specific set of tasks, habits, staff, skills, and tools when repeatedly leveraged, they systematically generate value.* "

Then, I always conclude, " *identifying them, using them as needed, this specific set of of tasks, habits, staff, skills and tools is a fantastic source of growth and wealth for the business.* "

The value chain is a very powerful tool, it allows businesses to analyze, understand, and improve the way they create value. The GAFAs dominate digital business because, they know, understand, and rely on their value chain to thrive.

The lesson the value chain model teaches is about business transformation. It teaches that, business transformation so many IT leaders fear is about adjusting or optimizing a small piece, the most strategic piece of your business: its value chain.

The reason is simple, the bottom line of every single business is to generate value, focusing on the value chain to optimize it is the most effective way to make your business competitive and wealthy. That's my over 20 years experience helping businesses transform.

The Strategic Role of DevOps

The fact you must be aware of is, DevOps plays a strategic role in the company's digital success.

DevOps is strategic for two fundamental reasons:

- It's the enabler of the company's network effects
- And more importantly, it's the new value chain

Let's discuss them.

How DevOps Enables Network Effects

Most IT experts ignore it, the reason why DevOps is essential to any successful digital business is, it enables companies' network effects. That's what figures 16 demonstrates.

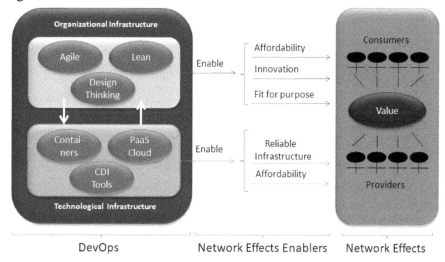

Figure 16 - DevOps as the enabler of the network effects

As illustrated, to create powerful network effects there are at least five conditions to meet. They're actually the platform consumers and providers expectations, they include:

- Affordability of the services consumed by consumers
- Innovation of the services consumed by consumers
- The « fit for purpose » nature of the services consumed by consumers
- Reliability of the infrastructure offered to providers

- Affordability of the infrastructure offered to providers

The organizational and technological infrastructures of DevOps offer several enablers that help to meet the five fundamental conditions.

How Agile Enables Responsiveness

When Agile philosophy and practices are properly enforced, they create across the organization's value chain the conditions that make the company responsive to consumers and providers expectations.

Methodologies - Scrum

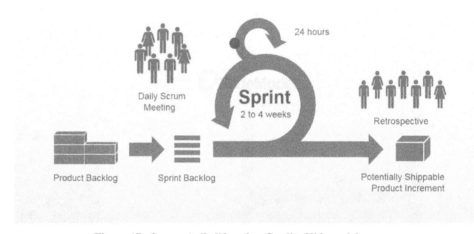

Figure 17 - Scrum Agile lifecycle - Credit: Slidemodel.com

As illustrated by the Scrum agile lifecycle, agile simplifies the company's operational interactions and as a result introduces a collaborative mindset that accelerates problem solving and decision making.

How Lean Enables Responsiveness

When Lean philosophy and practices are enforced and properly adopted, they widespread across the organization's value chain to create the conditions that make the company services affordable to consumers.

Figure 18 - Lean principles

As illustrated, in addition to keeping the organization's staff focused on continuously increasing customer value, Lean practices stress the continuous elimination of waste as well as the improvement of operational practices.

As a result they reduce operational costs, allow low prices, and make the company's services affordable.

How Design Thinking Enables Innovation

When <u>Design Thinking</u> – human-centered approach to innovation focused on solving people problem – philosophy and practices are properly enforced and adopted, they widespread across the organization's value chain an innovation mindset.

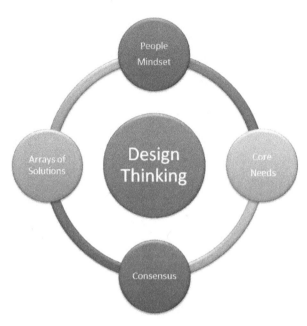

Figure 19 - Design Thinking principles

As illustrated, by seeking to understand the mindset of people the product is designed for, get a grasp of unmet needs, considering a wide and fresh array of solutions, and more importantly, not imposing a solution, design thinking increases the company's chances to continuously develop innovation.

How the Technological Infrastructure Enables Infrastructure Reliability

When they expected technology infrastructure are provided, they not only massively attract producers, but more importantly, they offer positive experience that keep them loyal.

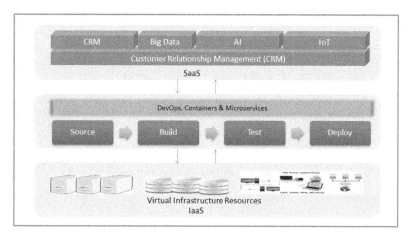

Figure 20 - DevOps Technological Infrastructure

As illustrated, by providing CD toolchain, Big Data, Artificial Intelligence (AI), Internet of Things (IoT) cloud-hosted infrastructure, not only offer what producers need from a technology perspective, but more importantly, take advantage of the cloud's cost savings to IT investments and reduce operational costs and as a result, make the company's infrastructure services affordable for producers.

Why DevOps is the Company's New Value Chain

Just like Michael Porter's value chain model enables the company's assets to generate value, DevOps offers the mechanisms that create or keep effective the company's network effects.

I guessed you got it, DevOps is the new value chain, you need it to succeed in today's network economy.

Now that we've seen the determinants of successful digital businesses – *internet business model, value chain, DevOps* – their purpose, their impacts, and how they work, we can discuss digital business architectures.

Let's start with the pipeline-based digital organization.

The Company Digital Transformation Continuum

Taking a company digital isn't the complex operation that many describe, we'll see it in the following sections.

However, it's a process that can be complex; it demands the use of the digital transformation continuum that I've developed. It's part of my consulting services.

Figure 21 - Company Digital Transformation Continuum

As the figure shows, it's a five-step process that includes *analyzing the market in which you do business, developing the digital strategy, developing the business model, clarifying the value chain,* and *implementing the DevOps capability.*

A variety of tools and methodologies facilitate each of step. Let's examine them.

Market Analysis

Market analysis seeks to spot opportunities and segments to focus on, it combines Michael Porter's *Five Forces* framework and *SWOT matrix.*

The primary challenge is to identify market trends and profitable opportunities.

I personally use Michael Porter's Five Forces and the SWOT matrix. Let's discuss them.

The *Five Forces framework* seeks to measure the competition intensity in your markets through assessing four fundamental issues including:

- Market new entrants
- Customers' bargaining power
- Providers' bargaining power
- And product substitutes

The following figure summarizes the logic of the five forces framework:

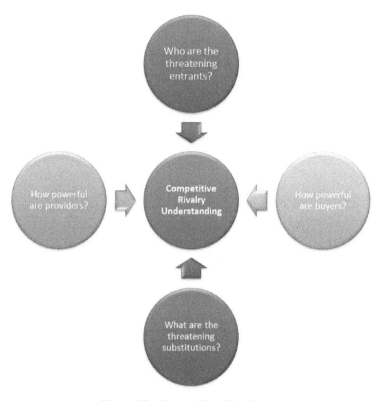

Figure 22 - Competition Five Forces

The framework is structured as a four-concern questionnaire including questions around the following:

- The threatening entrants entering the company's market
- The bargaining power of customers
- The threatening product substitutes brought in by new entrants
- The bargaining power of providers and vendors

The *SWOT matrix,* unlike the Five Forces framework, seeks to bring out the actions to take to adjust you digital strategy and meet your market competitive challenges.

Figure 23 - The SWOT Matrix

The matrix is structured as a four-concern questionnaire including questions around the following:

- The company's strengths versus its markets' threats and opportunities
- The company's weaknesses as to these sames threats and opportunities
- The markets' opportunities and threats

Digital Strategy Development

The development of digital strategy seeks to build the story about how the company will survive and thrive in its disrupted markets.

The stake is the clarification of the business objectives as well as the means – *value propositions underpinning the marketing strategy, key processes to focus on*, and *the organizational and technological infrastructure* –needed to achieve them.

The *Strategy Map* is the tool I use to help businesses develop and execute their digital strategy. It's a collaborative tool which seeks to help executive teams agree on objectives and get a consensus on the means – *human*, *practices*, and *technology* – to achieve them.

The following figure gives an example of strategy map.

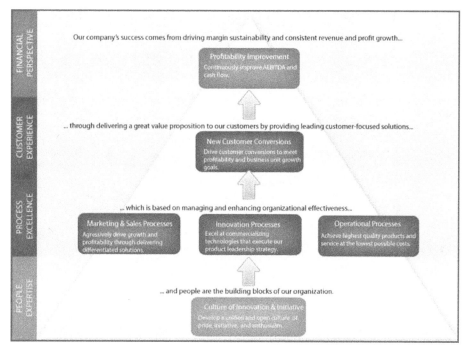

Figure 24 - Strategy Map - Credit: OnStrategy

The framework is structured in a two-part questionnaire including including the *strategy's objective* which is concerned with the financial and customer perspectives and the *strategy's drivers* which is concerned with the internal and learning & growth perspectives.

The questions revolve around the following:

- Financial perspective – What are the financial objectives of the digital strategy?
- Customer experience – What are the customer objectives of the digital strategy e.g., segments, value propositions, experience?
- Process excellence – What key processes — business and IT — should be stressed to achieve the objectives
- People expertise – What people and skills, value and beliefs, organizational and technological infrastructure can help?

Business Model Development

The business model development seeks to elaborate on the digital strategy by aggregating into an operational plan, the objectives, the needed value propositions, the key processes to focus on, and the organizational and technological infrastructure to invest in.

The top challenge is to put together the digital strategy elements into an actionable operational plan.

The *Business Model Canvas* is the framework I leverage, its purpose is to help executive teams to elaborate on the elements of digital strategies.

The following figure provides an overview of the business model canvas:

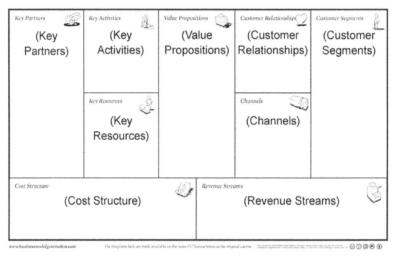

Figure 25 - Business Model Canvas - Credit: Alex Cowan

The framework is structured in a nine-topic questionnaire including questions around:

- Key partners – Who do we need to partner with to achieve our objectives.
- Key activities – What added-value activities make up our key processes?
- Key resources – What added-value resources — staff and skills, processes and practices, tools and technology — do we need?
- Value propositions – How relevant are the selected value propositions for our marketing strategy?
- Customer relationships – How should we manage relationships with customers in a way that generates value?
- Channels – What channels should we stress to make sure we're reaching relevant customer segments?
- Customer segments – What customer segments are relevant to our business?
- Cost structure – What's the best cost structure for our business?

- Revenue streams – What are our revenue streams?

Value Chain Identification

The bottom line in this step is to get across the company, a consensus on the added-value activities to consider as part of the value chain.

The challenge is to get a consensus on the added-value staff and skills, processes and practices, values and beliefs, and tools and infrastructure.

I use the value chain model to select and consolidate the added-value resources that'll support the digital business.

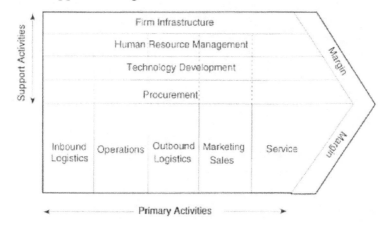

Figure 26 - Value chain model

The framework is structured in a nine-topic questionnaire including questions around:

- Firm infrastructure – What activities in the area of firm infrastructed should we selected as bringing value?
- Human resource management – What activities in the domain of HR should we consider added-value?
- Technology Development – What activities in research and development (R&D) can we selected as added-value?
- Procurement – What activities in the area of purchase should we select as added-value?
- Inboud Logistics – What activities in the supply chain domain should we consider added-value?
- Operations – What production activities should we select as bringing added-value?
- Outbound Logistics – What activities in the distribution domain should we consider added-value?

- Marketing & Sales – What marketing and sales activities should we select as adding value?
- Services – What activities in post sale area should we consider added-value?

DevOps Implementation

The objective in this critical step is to deploy DevOps' organizational and technological infrastructure.

There are two primary challenges including the implementation of the DevOps' technological infrastructure as the company's platform and getting DevOps culture adopted across the company.

Chapters 7, 8, and 8 will give you details about DevOps implementation. Patience.

The intent of the *The Company Digital Transformation Section* was to give you, gradually, understanding of the logic, principles, and tools needed to take a business digital.

Let's see now, how the digital transformation continuum helps to transform pipeline-based and platform-based digital organizations.

The Pipeline-Based Digital Organization

The architecture of the successful digital organization sends a proven message, *"without a proper business model, expecting to survive and thrive is a wishful thinking."*

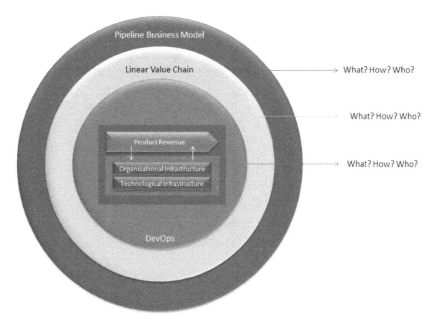

Figure 27 - Architecture of the pipeline-based digital organization

Let's discuss the pipeline-based digital organization and then the platform-based organization.

Clarifying Your Pipeline Business Model

The bottom line here is to imagine and then design a way of doing business that'll help the company succeed online.

The challenge is to understand the e-commerce ecosystem and spot the proper opportunities and associated market segments as well as the means —staff, providers, partners, organizational structure, technology infrastructure — required to succeed online.

The pipeline model development practice extends the *Business Model Canvas* questionnaire defined in the previous sections with the following concerns:

- Increasing the e-commerce website *traffic*
- Developing online partnerships example *affiliate programs*
- Ensuring data, identification, and traffic *security*
- Developing effective *content marketing*
- Ensuring positive *customer experience*
- *Innovating* in all aspects of the business

Optimizing Your Value Chain

The focus here is to select added-value elements — activities, staff, consumers, producers, processes, practices, values, beliefs, and more — identified in the business model to consolidate them into a value chain.

The challenge is to, not only spot the added-value elements of the business model, but also to aggregate them into a smart system that monetizes the business.

The principle is to make sure the concerns listed in the above section are part of the company's online value chain. They include:

- Website traffic optimization
- Partnerships development
- Cyber security management
- Content marketing
- Customer experience continuous improvement
- Innovation management

Deploying DevOps Entirely

The objective is to deploy the organizational and technological infrastructure of DevOps as the foundation of the organization's value chain.

The stake is to deploy DevOps in its entirety – *organizational and technological infrastructures* – and get it adopted across the business, particularly within the value chain.

Chapters 7, 8, and 9 detail all aspects of DevOps deployment from the organizational and infrastructure deployments to the adoption of changes.

The Platform-Based Digital Organization

Let's discuss the design of the platform-based digital organization, the internet business model, the value chain, and the DevOps capability.

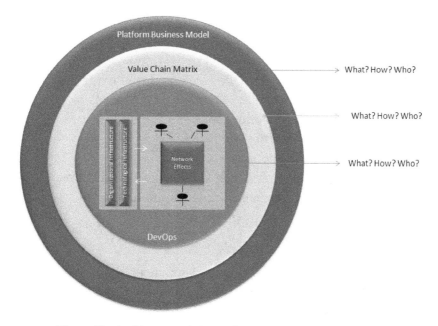

Figure 28 - Architecture of the platform-based digital organization

Clarifying The Platform Business Model

The objective is to imagine and then design a way of doing business that helps the company take advantage of powerful network effects.

The challenge is to properly use the platform business model as defined in chapter 2 to help the company not only fit in the network economy, but more importantly as said previously, take advantage of powerful network effects.

The platform model development practice extends on the *Business Model Canvas* questionnaire with the following additional concerns:

- Optimizing the company's *network effects*
- Optimizing interactions across the *platform*
- Monetizing *interactions* for producers and consumers
- Optimizing producers and consumers *experience*
- *Innovating* in all aspects of the business

Optimizing Your Value Chain Matrix

Like for the pipeline model, the objective is to select added-value elements – *activities, staff, consumers, producers, processes, practices, values, beliefs,* and *more* – identified in the business model and consolidate them into value chain.

The challenge is to, not only spot the added-value elements of the business model, but also to aggregate them into a way that creates network effects and generate the value expected by consumers and producers.

The practice is to make sure the concerns listed in the above section are part of the company's online value chain. They include:

- Network effects optimization
- Interactions optimization
- Interactions monetization
- Consumers and producers experience optimization
- Customer experience continuous improvement
- Innovation management

Deploying DevOps Entirely

Like for the pipeline model, the objective is to deploy the organizational and technological infrastructure of DevOps as the foundation of the organization's value chain.

The challenge is to, not only deploy DevOps in its entirety and get it adopted across the business, particularly within the value chain, but also implement an infrastructure that monetizes consumer-producer interactions.

Chapters 7, 8, and 9 detail all aspects of DevOps deployment from the organizational and infrastructure deployments to the adoption of changes.

What You Must Keep in Mind

Making a business competitive and profitable in today's expanding network economy isn't as simple as migrating IT to the cloud and deploying the recent IT innovations.

Of course these IT innovations matter, without them, trying to compete with the GAFAs is a wishful thinking. However, that's one of the key messages of this book, these recent IT innovations, particularly the productivity they provide, isn't enough to survive and thrive.

You need to transform your business, I mean, adjust it to digital competition requirements.

The digital competition is an expanding reality, do not deny it, you may rush your company to bankruptcy. Think about what happened to Nine West Holdings, The Bon-Ton Stores, Toys R Us, Remington, Southeastern Grocers, Tops Markets, and recently Sears.

Rather, embrace the changes and think beyond IT, think business transformation. It has nothing to do with the risky organizational upheaval many are talking about; as discussed in this chapter, it's about transforming a small piece of your organization: the *Value Chain*.

As you know it now, DevOps is the new value chain, transforming the value chain is about deploying it entirely, I mean, the technological infrastructure and the organizational infrastructure.

7. DevOps for Digital Service Development (BlueBird)

As we've seen in the previous chapters, providing innovations to keep the company's network effects positive is vital to your business lines.

The challenge is to continuously and rapidly deliver disruptive innovations, to resist the GAFAs' competition, survive, and thrive.

Your business lines will struggle to achieve that, unless they use a comprehensive digital products and services development platform.

Such platforms are thought to optimize and accelerate from the people, organizational, operational and technological perspectives, the design, development, testing, and deployment of disruptive innovations.

The DevOps for Digital Service Development (referred to as BlueBird) platform described in this chapter illustrates the functions, features, and benefits of such platforms.

This chapter covers:

- Challenges of today's digital services development
- Making the case for the BlueBird platform
- The BlueBird platform Microservices architecture
- Nuts and bolts of the BlueBird platform implementation

Challenges of Today's Digital Services Development

Business and IT leaders' lack of interest in the rising digital economy is a major concern; they either underestimate it or ignore it.

Obviously, the problems – *market share loss* and *bankruptcy* – faced by global companies like Toys R Us, and recently Sears didn't convince them to start their digital transformation.

They're wrong, if they don't offer digital products and services helpful to compete with the GAFAs' offerings, they will simply go bankrupt. That's what happened to Toys R Us.

The problem is, today's digital service development practices aren't mature. In fact, because they rely on enterprise data and applications, they're developed and managed using traditional software development approaches.

Despite commonalities between enterprise applications and digital services – *they're all based on software and leverage software development life cycle (SDLC)* – digital services have more complex requirements, and more importantly, more technological and technical challenges.

How to deliver more innovations, cheaper, and faster in a way that increases market shares and generates substantial revenue? That's the obsession of many business line leaders. The answer is, the BlueBird platform.

Making the Case for the BlueBird Platform

The Challenges of Today's New Product Development (NPD) Platforms

Two interrelated weaknesses prevent today's NPD platforms from helping business lines properly compete with the GAFAs. These weaknesses are:

- The inappropriate application of project management (PM) techniques to digital services development
- Business lines' disconnection from the stakes of the rising digital competition

The problems with the application of PM techniques is, despite helping monitoring product performances using financial portfolio management mechanisms, they narrow digital services development to a matter of properly planning and driving the implementation effort.

What the PM approach is blamed for is, it doesn't address issues as vital as innovation, responsiveness to market opportunities, and more importantly, it ignores the organizational and operational aspects of the digital service development effort.

Traditional product development platforms aren't only resource and time consuming, they're disconnected from the stakes of the network economy.

The Key Things to Know About the BlueBird Platform

The BlueBird platform extends the traditional notion of service development platform beyond tools and technology concerns.

It combines human, organizational, operational, and technological considerations to systemically deliver more innovations, cheaper and faster.

BlueBird is a DevOps-based platform for accelerated digital services design, development and deployment.

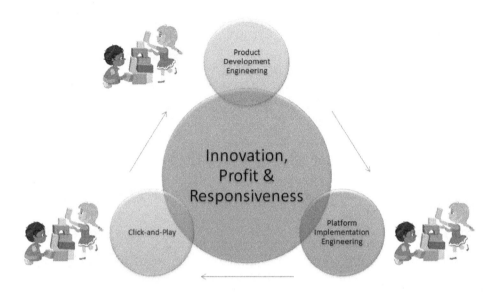

Figure 29 - Principles of the BlueBird platform

As the figure illustrates, the platform builds on three dimensions supporting the digital service development process. They make it essential to survive and thrive in disrupted markets, they include:

- Accelerated platform implementation
- The click-and-play feature
- Digital product engineering

Let's discuss them.

Facilitating and Accelerating the Platform Implementation

The **platform implementation engineering** dimension as its name suggests, provides a comprehensive and automated process that makes easy and accelerates its deployment.

There are two fundamental elements:

- The automation and rapid deployment of the organizational and technological infrastructure
- The digital services development work environment

The complete services development work environment refers to the organizational and technological infrastructures provided by the BlueBird.

The Vital Role of the Click-and-Play Feature

The **Click-and-Play** (CnP) feature makes the platform easy to deploy; it makes the platform totally operational in a couple of minutes after two to three mouse clicks.

It reduces the burden on companies by providing a mechanism that drastically simplifies the organizational and technological infrastructure deployment process.

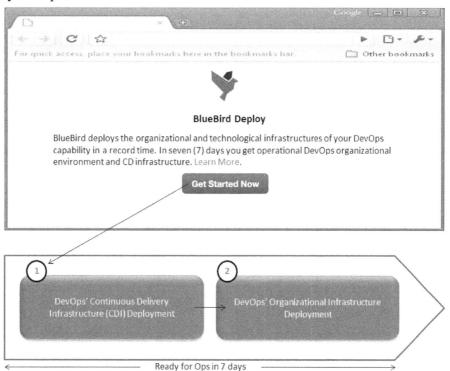

Figure 30 - Deploying an Operational DevOps Capability in One Click

No human intervention is needed, in one click, you get an operational CDI, and more importantly, all the resources needed to start right away, the adoption of DevOps in your organization.

Accelerating Design and Development with Product Engineering

The **product development engineering dimension** builds on Design Thinking, DevOps, and Agile practices to address the organizational and operational aspects of the digital service development effort.

The combination of these practices creates a climate and environment conducive for developing and deploying evermore innovations, faster, and cost-effectively.

The BlueBird Platform Microservices Architecture

What are the building blocks of the BlueBird platform? How do they connect to enable disruptive innovations development? Are some of the questions you may have in mind. This section provides the answers.

The BlueBird Platform Architecture

Four fundamental building blocks make up the BlueBird platform, they enable accelerated innovations design, development, and deployment.

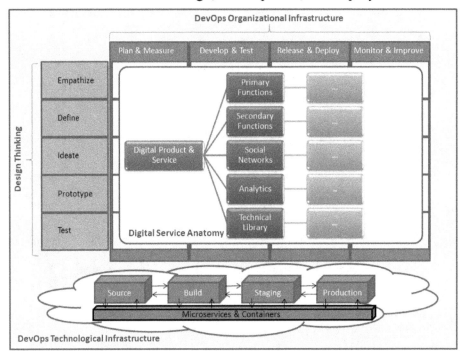

Figure 31 - The high level architecture of the BlueBird platform

The platform distinguishes between intangible build blocks – *DevOps' Organizational Infrastructure, Digital Service Breakdown structure* and *Design Thinking* – and tangible ones including *DevOps' Technological Infrastructure* also known as the *Continuous Delivery Pipeline*.

Let's discuss them.

The DevOps' Organizational Infrastructure

Delivering the right disruptive innovations in a timely manner is the competitive bottom line. Without that competitive advantage, chances are your business lines go through terrible troubles.

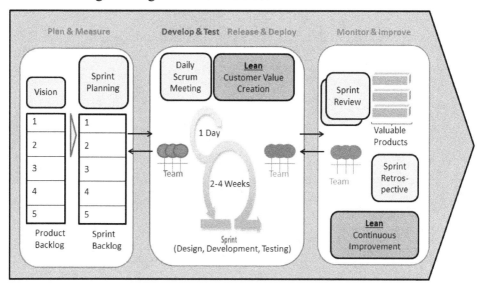

Figure 32 – Scrum Deployed as the foundation of DevOps' organizational infrastructure

DevOps' organizational infrastructure is based on *Scrum Agile* and takes advantage of three elements to make the development activity flexible and responsive. They include:

- Agile practices
- Lean practices
- And the scrum agile lifecycle

How DevOps Uses Agile to Create the Conditions for Velocity, Responsiveness, and Innovation

Agile through its values and principles creates the conditions for innovation, responsiveness, fast time-to-market, and accelerated time-to-revenue.

The exhibit below summarizes the agile contributions:

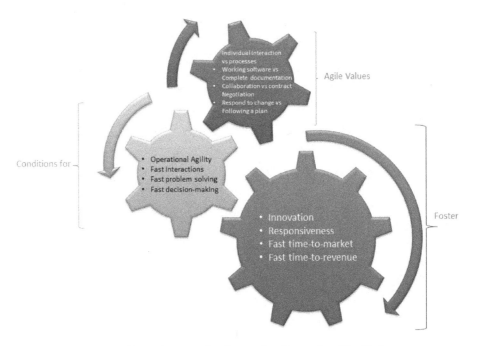

Figure 33 - Agile Contributions to DevOps and to BlueBird

The story told by the exhibit is, Agile fundamental values – *Individuals and Interactions Over Processes and Tools, Working Software Over Comprehensive Documentation, Customer Collaboration Over Contract Negotiation, and Responding to Change Over Following a Plan* – create the conditions for innovation, responsiveness, fast time-to-market and time-to-revenue.

These conditions include organizational and operational agility, accelerated staff interactions, fast problem solving and decision-making across the organization's value chain.

The following table provides the top Agile methodologies and tools you can invest in to support your value chain:

Methodologies	Tools	Comments
SCRUM	- Jira Software - GitHub	Scrum, as the top agile methodology, is used to work on complex projects and is focused on the faster delivery of high-quality software.
Extreme Programming (XP)	- ExtremePlanner - Project Planning & Tracking System (PPTS)	XP is an agile project management methodology, a framework which is set to improve software quality and responsiveness to changing customer requirements. Another advantage of XP is in simplifying and speeding up the process of developing new software, so the product would be launched promptly with a solid MVP.
Kanban	- Jira Software - LiquidPlanner - Proggio	Kanban is the second agile framework used. It's based on three principles: - to visualize what you plan to do today (workflow) - to limit the number of tasks in progress for balance the flow-based approach - and not to forget to enhance flow

Figure 34 - Top Agile methodologies and tools you can invest in

Why Understanding Michael Porter's Value Chain is Vital

The second element of the DevOps component to consider, in reality the most important is the value stream; it's addressed in this book as the value chain.

The value chain refers to the set of added-value – only added-value – staff and skills, interactions and activities, and processes and activities specifically mobilized across the organization to create business value.

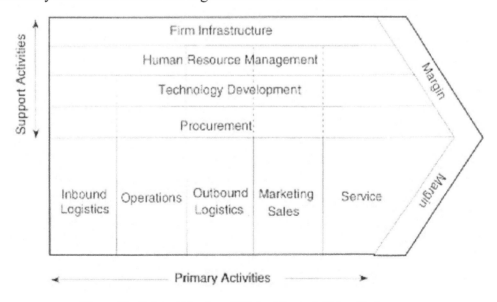

Figure 35 - Original Version of Michael Porter's Value Chain

The concept (which became a tool) was popularized by Harvard's business strategy professor, Michael Porter in his best seller, *The Competitive Advantage* in 1985.

The purpose of the model was to provide businesses with a tool that helps to understand the mechanisms underlying their value creation process, analyze them, and improve them.

As the picture shows, the original value chain consists of five primary and four support added-value activities. Primary activities are directly concerned with the creation and delivery of value through product and service developments.

Support activities helps to run the business but arent't directly related to the creation of value and associated products and services.

How DevOps Uses the Notion of Value Stream to Organize and Boost Value Delivery

The value chain model has influenced almost all the methodologies, works and disciplines related to the improvement of business operational performance ranging from Process Reengineering and Total Quality Management (TQM) to Capability Maturity Model Integration (CMMI) and Information Technology Infrastructure (ITIL).

The philosophy and principles of the model were reused under the names of *Value Stream* and *Value Stream Mapping* in the Lean Manufacturing methodology invented by Toyota in the early 1990s.

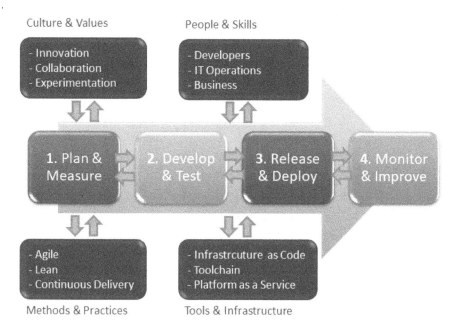

Figure 36 - The DevOps Value Stream

The concept of value chain and its derivatives the value stream and value stream mapping are an integral part of DevOps and BlueBird.

The value stream mapping is the Lean tool Toyota used to define and optimize the various steps involved in designing, developing, testing and deploying products or services.

The following table provides three of some of the top value streaming mapping (VSM) tools:

VSM Tools	Companies	Description
Lucidchart	Lucidchart	Lucidchart features a drang-and-drop interface and real-time collaboration capabilities. In addition to working on major operating systems, Lucidchart is also functional on the iPad through an optimized iPad application. On the iPad, Lucidchart allows users to touch-draw shapes which are automatically converted to standard symbols.
Easy VSM Tools	SmartDraw	SmartDraw's exclusive automation technology built into a value stream mapping template applies the Lean approach to value stream maps, reducing time and effort to create a VSM.
Electronic VSM (eVSM)	eVSM	eVSM allows easy capture of a wall VSM (value stream map) into electronic format for sharing, fast visual analysis of the waste, and focused selection of improvement ideas through what-if analysis. It has unique capability and a set of wizards to simplify VSM related calculations for each industry/VSM type.

Figure 37 - Three of the Top VSM tools you can invest in

How DevOps Leverages Lean Production to Ensure Business Value

The last piece of the DevOps component to consider is the Lean practice. Fundamentally, Lean is a systematic method for waste minimization within a manufacturing system without sacrificing productivity.

Figure 38 - Lean Manufacturing Workflow - Credit: Croz.net

It takes into account waste created through overburden and waste created through unevenness in work loads.

Addressing issues from the client's perspective, Lean's philosophy assumes that, the client consumes a product or service thought, designed, developed, and deployed with processes designed to deliver a specific value he/she is willing to pay for.

Lean manufacturing makes obvious what adds value, by reducing everything else. DevOps uses the Lean principles as the enablers of customer value creation.

The following table provides three of the top Lean production and management tools you can invest in:

Lean Tools	Description
5S	5S is a workplace organization method that involves 5 phases that happen to begin with the letter S in both Japanese and English. They are: seiri (sort), seiton (set), seiso (shine), seiketsu (standardize), and shitsuke (sustain). The 5S system improves workplace efficiency and eliminates waste. Managers and workers achieve greater organization, standardization, and efficiency while reducing costs and boosting productivity.
DMAIC	DMAIC (for Define, Measure, Analyze, Improve and Control) is an improvement cycle with five phases; define, measure, analyze, improve, control. These phases are used to help ensure that improvements are data-driven, measurable, and repeatable. DMAIC works to improve problem solving by providing structure to the task. Due to the fact that it is data-driven, it's easier to identify the appropriate targets and root causes and to make sure that any implemented changes get better results than the previous method.
Kanban	Kanban means "billboard" or "shop keeper's sign." It is a technique that Toyota executives developed after observing the visual clues that grocery store managers use to keep just the right level of inventory on hand. The idea is to maximize the flow of goods and work. It is achieved by ensuring that work is visualized, work-in-progress (WIP) is limited, flow is not interrupted and that improvement is continuous.

Figure 39 - Top Lean tools you can invest in

Augmenting DevOps with Design Thinking Principles

That's my experience, I think what makes *Design Thinking* powerful is how it considers innovation; it doesn't see it from the distorted lenses of technology sophisticated features, but from the belief that, "*the people who face problem are the ones who hold the key to their problem's answer.*"

Used for the very first time by John E. Arnold in 1959 and then expanded by Rolf Faste on McKim's work at Standford University in the 1990s, *Design Thinking* is a human-focused problem solving approach which stresses:

- Empathy – The ability to understand and share the feelings of another
- Collaboration – Putting contributions together to produce value
- Co-creation – Economic strategy that brings different parties together in order to jointly produce a mutually valued outcome
- And stakeholder feedback

The combination of these elements unlocks creativity and innovation.

How Does It Work?

The secret of Design Thinking is its development lifecycle; it's thought to guarantee that each step in the development effort increases the chances of delivering the right solution.

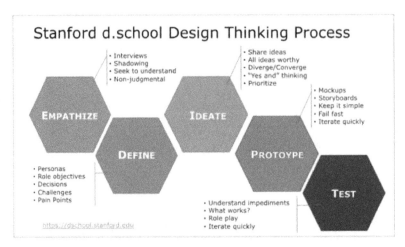

Figure 40 - Design Thinking Life Cycle - Credit: Standford University

Design Thinking splits the innovation development effort in five steps including:

- Empathize
- Define
- Ideate
- Prototype
- And Test

Let's discuss them!

Empathize –The bottom line in this stage is to gain an empathic understanding of the problem to solve.

This stage is critical as it's where the design team is involved to find out more about the problem through observing, engaging and empathizing with people to understand their experiences and motivations.

Tools like Agile User Stories are leveraged to help gain a deeper understanding of the issues involved.

Empathy is critical as it allows, product designers to set aside their own assumptions about the world in order to gain insight into consumers and their needs.

Define – The purpose of this stage is to put together the information created and collected during the Empathize step.

It's where the collected observations are collaboratively analyzed and summarized to clearly define the core problems.

The design team uses tools like *Use Case Diagram* to collaboratively gather great ideas and bring out features, functions, and any other elements likely to solve the problems.

Ideate – It's where ideas are generated based on the human-centered problem statement defined in Define stage.

This stage is of importance because it's where the design team start to think outside the box to identify innovative solutions to the problem statement or to look for alternative ways of viewing the problem.

Ideation techniques such as <u>Brainstorm</u>, <u>Brainwrite</u>, and <u>Worst Possible Idea</u>, are used to facilitate and accelerate the identification of solutions.

Prototype – The purpose here is to produce a number of inexpensive prototypes of the product and specific features found within the product, so they can investigate the solutions generated in the Define and Ideate stages.

It's an in-house experimental phase, and the goal is to identify the best possible solution for each of the problems identified during the first three steps.

The solutions are implemented within prototypes, and they're experimented and either accepted, improved and re-examined, or rejected on the basis of the users' experiences. The design team as well as a panel of business and IT staff are involved in the process.

At the end of this stage, the design team has a better idea of the operational, technical, and technological constraints of the digital product and have a greater perspective of how users would behave, think, and feel when interacting with it.

Test –The objective in this final stage is to rigorously test the digital product to redefine problems and inform the understanding of the users.

This is iterative process is executed through pilot experiment projects under actual business conditions involving a panel of business and IT staff as well as well-selected user groups.

Even during this test phase, changes and refinements are made in order to rule out problem solutions and derive as deep an understanding of the product and its users as possible.

Why Augmenting DevOps with Design Thinking Principles Makes the Business a Disruptor?

Using the tools and methodologies specifically thought and tailored to address innovations development is essential to meet your disrupted market challenges. That's where Design Thinking brings value to DevOps.

As the exhibit shows, augmenting DevOps with Design Thinking principles create a combination of factors that make the company a potential disruptor:

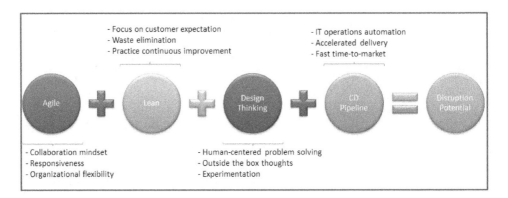

Figure 41 - How Design Thinking augments the disruption potential of DevOps

Agile practices through the collaboration mindset, responsiveness and organizational flexibility provide the organization with the responsiveness need to react to market opportunities.

Lean practices through the focus on customer value and continuous improvement of operational practices give the organization the innovation capacity it needs to create positive network effects.

Design Thinking by stressing customer-centered solution and outside the box thoughts gives the organization the innovation capacity to compete with the GAFAs and thrive in the network economy.

The CD Pipeline by automating IT delivery processes adds to the power of agile practices, and provides the organization with the responsiveness need to react to market opportunities.

The Digital Service Anatomy

Getting the big picture that not only simplifies complexity but also facilitates and accelerates the design, development, testing, and deployment of the digital service is a significant competitive advantage.

It's the purpose of the Digital Service Breakdown Structure, also referred to in this books as Digital Service Anatomy (DSA).

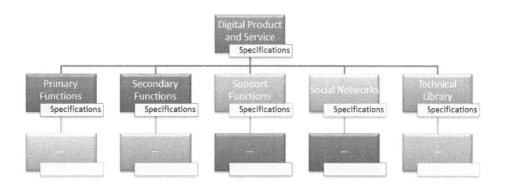

Figure 42 - Digital Service Breakdown Structure Level 1

As the exhibit shows, it's an effective tool that highlights and specifies the functions, and the physical and technical components of a particular digital service under consideration.

Each function or component at the first level of the hierarchy breaks down into subfunctions or sub-component with the associated specifications.

Let's detail them!

Primary and Secondary Functions

Having clear ideas about the value expected by customers and understanding the mechanisms to enable them are two essential conditions for successful disruptive digital services.

That's what the *Primary Functions* and *Secondary Functions* branches of the DSA seek to achieve.

As illustrated, primary and secondary functions respectively break down into primary and secondary items labeled in the picture PF1 and SF1.

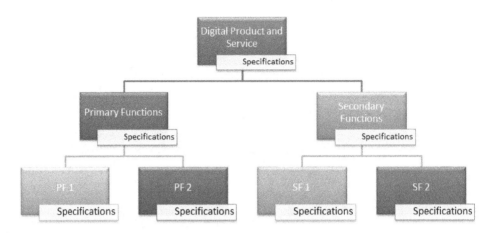

Figure 43 - Primary and Secondary Functions Branches

The purpose of the **Primary Functions** is to enable the core benefits of the digital service. Example, placing or receiving calls, sending or receiving texts, and sending or receiving emails are some of the primary functions of the iPhone.

Secondary Functions support the benefits considered not essential but helpful by customers. Examples of secondary functions of the iPhone include calendar, calculator, electronic book reader, weather forecaster, and more.

Support Functions

Making sure customers make an optimal use of the digital service should be your permanent concern. It's the customer's primary concern anyway.

That's the purpose of the *Support Functions* branch of the DSA.

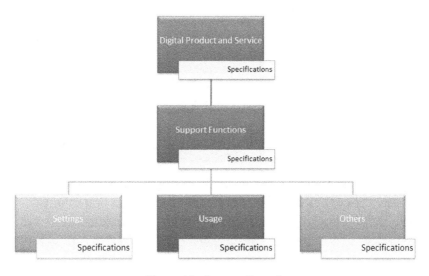

Figure 44 - Support Branch

Let's take a look at some of the usual support functions!

Settings enable features likely to improve the customer's experience with the digital service. The fundamental goal is to make him loyal.

Examples include cranking up and down brightness, disabling push email, turning on Do Not Disturb, tweaking the size of text, configuring auto-lock, and more like it.

Social Networks

Social networks have become essential communication, information, and promotion spaces for businesses. They are integral parts of any digital service.

It's the purpose of the *Social Networks* branch of the DSA.

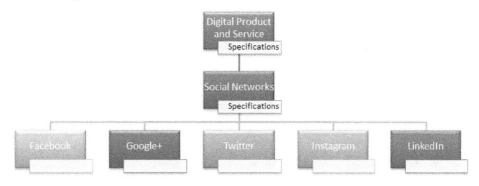

Figure 45 - The Social Network Branch

Let's see how they contribute to the digital service competitiveness!

Facebook function, as suggested, gives access to that social networking website where users can post comments, share photographs and videos, and post links to news or other interesting content on the web, chat live, and watch short-form video. Users can even order food on it.

Shared content can be made publicly accessible, or it can be shared only among a select group of friends or family, or with a single person.

Google+ function as you've guessed it, gives access to Google's social networking platform.

Basically, Google Plus is an interest-based platform where like-minded individuals communicate, collaborate and create as a community.

Unlike other social media networks, this platform gives you an unparalleled opportunity to forge meaningful, long-term relationships by consistently engaging with peers and other industry experts.

Twitter function as you've guessed it, gives access to the known micro-blogging site. Posting a message is known as a tweet. People make connections by following other people's twitter feeds. Once you click follow, anything that person or organisation says will appear on your timeline.

LinkedIn function gives access to that social network specifically designed for career and business professionals to connect. LinkedIn is about building strategic relationships.

Technical Library

Ensuring the digital service development team's productivity through concentrating and giving easy access to the needed methodologies, technologies, and tools is an obligation. It's the purpose of the *Technical Library*.

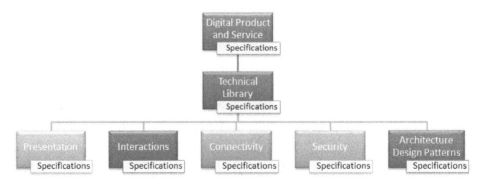

Figure 46 - DSA's Technical Library

Let's see their role in the digital service development process!

Presentation – When you interact with the digital service web interface — Laptop, Mobile, ATM — you're interacting with the presentation layer code. The presentation code controls web user interactions with the digital service and its appearance. It contains both view:

- Elements – layouts, blocks, templates
- And controllers which process commands to and from the user interface

It builds on HTML, CSS, and HTML solutions to make the customer experience as superior as possible.

Connectivity – Refers to the set of solutions and technologies connecting digital services to each other or to external devices across the internet in order to transfer data back and forth.

Security – Refers to the set of cybersecurity practices, solutions, and technologies leveraged to protect the services against digital attacks.

It ensures the integrity, confidentiality and availability of data and information handled across the internet by the digital service.

Design Patterns – are reusable solutions to frequent digital service design challenges. They're digital service design helpers.

They provide directions for accelerating design, development, and testing and describe the service's component structure, relationships, and interactions.

Microservices-Oriented Specifications

Clearly and accurately defining and describing the functions, features, and behaviours of the digital service is the primary key success factors.

Specifications are the central element of the DSA, they build on the microservices philosophy to describe the functions, features and behavior of the digital service to design, develop, test, and deploy.

They're the fundamental tool of the design team. The following exhibit depicts the digital service's specification structure and content:

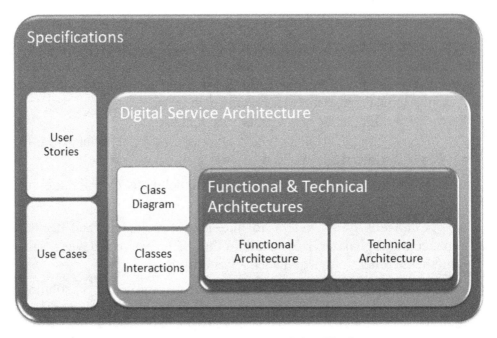

Figure 47 - Digital Service Compenent's Specifications

As suggested by the picture, the microservices-based digital service specifications organizes the design process in three steps including:

- Capturing the user perspective
- Deriving the developer perspective from the user perspective
- And defining the service architect perspective

Let's discuss them starting with the user perspective!

The *User Perspective* is captured through two tools including the *User Stories* and the *Use Cases*.

User Stories – As seen previously, innovations are based on core customer needs and wants. Properly capturing them is the first step towards successful disruptive services.

It's the purpose of the user story illustrated in the following figure:

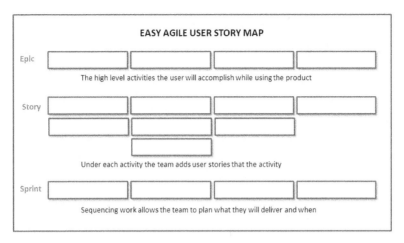

Figure 48 – User story map used at WellBeing

The user story is an Agile software development tool that describes the type of user, what they want and why.

It helps the design team to collaboratively create a simplified description of a business or customer requirement.

Use Cases – Identifying the digital service's use cases, in other words the functions intended to deliver the benefits expected by customers is the second step towards successful disruptive services.

It's the objective of the use case tool illustrated in the following exhibit:

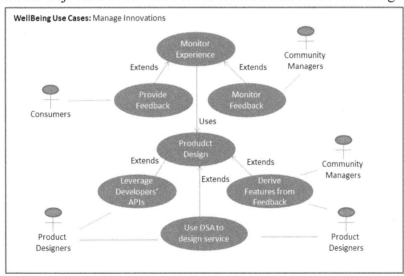

Figure 49 – WellBeing innovation management use cases

It shows the stakeholders involved in WellBeing's innovation management activities, they include consumers, APIs developers, product designers, and community managers.

It also highlights "*Monitor Experience*" and "*Product Design*" as the primary processes as well as the stakeholders interacting with them.

The *Developer Perspective* is captured using two different tools including *Class Diagram and Collaboration Diagram.*

Class Diagram – Identifying and modeling the elements that make up the digital service as well as with the business rules that relate them is the third step towards successful disruptive innovations.

That's the purpose of the class diagram illustrated in the exhibit below:

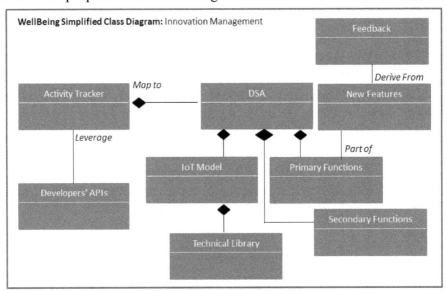

Figure 50 - WellBeing innovation management class diagram

This very simplified class diagram highlights the business rules and business objects underpinning the software supporting the benefits delivered by WellBeing's activity tracker.

It also shows that activity tracker class maps to the digital server anatomy (DSA) to deliver the expected benefits and that the DSA builds on an Internet of Things (IoT) model to technically implement desired features.

Activity tracker new features are derived from consumers' feedback and are part of its primary functions.

The varied classes are instanciated into objects which hold the data and functions needed to deliver the expected benefits.

Collaboration diagram – Modeling how the elements that make up the digital service interact to deliver the expected benefits is the fourth step towards disruptive innovations.

It's the objective of the collaboration diagram illustrated in the following exhibit:

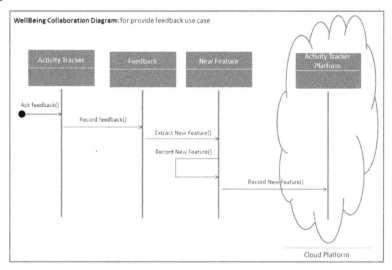

Figure 51 – Object Interactions specifying the "Provide Feedback" use case

It depicts the interactions that'll take place within the software to support the "provide feedback" use case.

(1) The activity tracker's interface uses the *AcknowledgeFeedback()* method to acknowledge consumer's feedback **(2)** then invokes Feedback object's *RecordFeedback()* method to record the feedback. **(3)** New Feature object's *ExtractNewFeature()* method is used to extract features from the feedback and **(4)** then recorded via the *RecordNewFeature()*.

The *Service Architect Perspective* is captured using *the Functional Architecture* and *Technical Architecture* tools.

Functional and Microservices Architecture – Providing and sharing the big picture of the future digital service from its functions perspective is the fourth step towards successful disruptive innovations.

It's the purpose of the functional architecture diagram illustrated in the following picture:

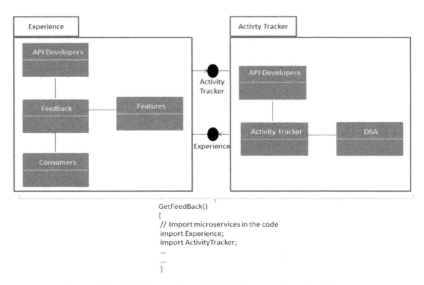

Figure 52 – WellBeing Simplified Microservices Architecture

This simplified diagram summarizes WellBeing' logical software architecture supporting the company's innovation management policy.

WellBeing builds on two categories of reusable objects, their functions, the data they hold as well as their interactions. These categories include:

- The "*Experience*" package concerned with managing the consumers' experience with the company's products
- And "*Activity Tracker*" package focused on activity trackers' architecture and features

Each package offers two microservices – Activity Tracker and Experience – in the form of interfaces imported and invoked in the digital service's software code to enable the expected functions, features, and behaviors.

Technical and Container Architecture – Mapping the Package Diagram's packages and embedded objects to the technologies likely to support their implementation is the fifth step towards successful disruptive innovations.

It's the purpose of the Technical architecture illustrated in the following picture:

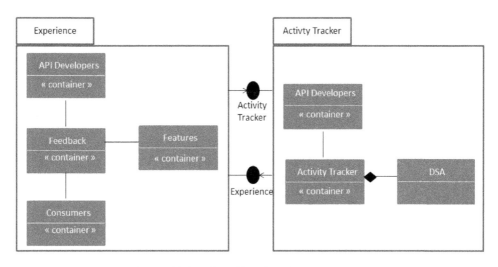

Figure 53 – WellBeing Simplified Container Architecture

The objectives is to map functional packages into Microservices supported by Docker containers.

The exhibit highlights the fact that WellBeing's digital services build on a microservices architecture to deliver the expected benefits.

The Continuous Delivery Pipeline

Building on a toolchain that automates the key service design, development, and deployment processes and tasks brings speed, velocity, and responsiveness to your digital service development capability.

It's the purpose of the DevOps Continuous Delivery Pipeline represented in the following exhibit:

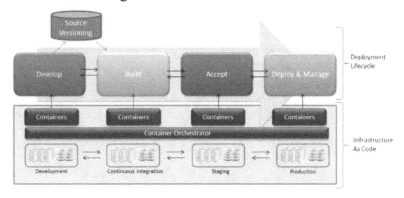

Figure 54 - DevOps Continuous Delivery Pipeline

As illustrated, the delivery pipeline is composed of four technology stacks, each stack enable a specific step of the DevOps deployment lifecycle.

Let's discuss them!

Containers and Container Orchestrator

Containers are an approach that packages an application's code, its configurations, and dependencies into a standard unit of software for consistency, efficiency, productivity, and version control.

As you can see in the previous exhibit, at its simplest, a container-based infrastructure consists of three fundamental elements:

- The container
- The application
- And the container management system

Let's discuss them!

The container – It allows developers to easily package an application's code, configurations, and dependencies into easy to use building blocks that deliver environmental consistency, operational efficiency, developer productivity, and version control.

With containers, developers can code, test, and run their source codes without concern about the operating system (OS).

The application – It refers to the application's code, its configuration and dependencies packaged in the container.

The container management system – Also referred to as container orchestrator, it automates the coordination of software containers and provides mechanisms to manage automatically track and monitor software containers.

Development Technology Stack

Developing complex digital services in an fast competition context requires reliance on a technological platform that automates and accelerates development tasks as much as possible.

It's the role of the Integrated Development Environment (IDE).

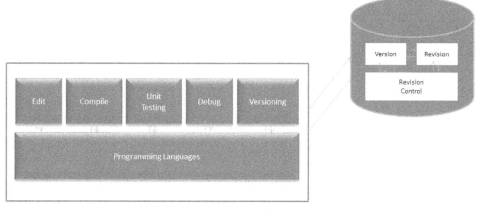

Figure 55 - Development Build Block

Integrated development environments (IDE) should be see as software development suites that consolidate basic tools required to write and test software. Developing software required tools that often include text editors, code libraries, compilers and test platforms.

Without IDEs, developers will have to select, deploy, integrate and manage all of these tools separately.

IDEs bring in many of those development-related tools together as a single framework, application or service.

They're designed to simplify software development and can identify and minimize coding mistakes and typos.

The following table lists some of top IDEs you can invest in:

IDE	Companies	Description
Microsoft Visual Studio	Microsoft	The many editions of this IDE are capable of creating all types of programs ranging from web applications to mobile apps to video games. This series of software includes tons of tools for compatibility testing so that you can see how your apps run on more than 300 devices and browsers. Thanks to its flexibility, Visual Studio is a great tool for both students and professionals.
Eclipse	Open Source	Eclipse is a free and flexible open source editor useful for beginners and pros alike. Eclipse has a wide range of capabilities thanks to a large number of plug-ins and extensions. In addition to debugging tools and Git/CVS support, the standard edition comes with Java and Plugin Development Tooling. The Eclipse Marketplace Client gives users access to a treasure trove of plugins and information supplied by an expanding community of developers.
NetBeans	Open Source	NetBeans is a free and open-source IDE. Ideal for editing existing projects or starting from scratch, NetBeans boasts a simple drag-and-drop interface that comes with a myriad of convenient project templates. It is primarily used to develop Java applications, but you can download bundles that support other languages.

Figure 56 - Top IDEs you can invest in

Build Technology Stack

Anticipating and getting feedback on code defects to proactively correct them and keep going the development and deployment processes is essential to deliver more innovations, cheaper, and faster. That's why relying on a continuous integration (CI) platform matters.

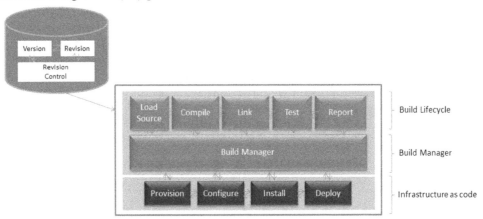

Figure 57 - Build Technology Stack

Build Manager (or orchestrator) is the central element of the CI platform.

The Build Manager assembles all the components of a software application into an installable software product.

As the exhibit shows, he leverages a build lifecycle to continuously tracks new versions of the software and perform the following tasks:

- Gathering of the source code
- Compilation or interpretation of the source code
- Unit testing of the source code
- Build and test notifications

Build managers take advantage of infrastructure as code mechanisms to provision as needed and configure the required resources – servers, networking, storage, and more.

The following table lists some of the top CI platforms you can invest in:

CI Tools	Companies	Description
Jenkins	Open Source	Jenkins is the number one open-source project for automating your projects. With thousands of plugins to choose from, Jenkins can help teams to automate any task that would otherwise put a time-consuming strain on your software team. Common uses include building projects, running tests, bug detection, code analysis, and project deployment.
Travis	Travis CI	Travis CI is a CI platform that automates the process of software testing and deployment of applications. It's built as a platform that integrates with your GitHub projects so that you can start testing your code on the fly. With customers like Facebook, Mozilla, Twitter, Heroku, and others, it's one of the leading continuous integration tools on the market.
GitLab CI	GitLab	GitLab is a rapidly growing code management platform for the modern developer. It provides tools for issue management, code views, continuous integration and deployment, all within a single dashboard. GitLab ships pre-built packages for popular Linux distributions, it installs in minutes, has a friendly UI, and offers detailed documentation on every feature.

Figure 58 - Top CI Tools you can invest in

Acceptance Test Technology Stack

Making sure in production-like environments, from the customer perspective that, digital services won't fail in a way that affect loyalty to company's brand is vitally important.

It's the purpose of the staging test platform.

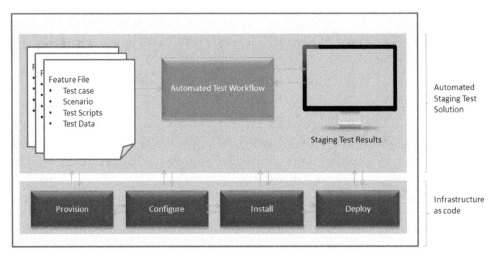

Figure 59 - Acceptance Test Technology Stack

Automated Staging Test (AST) solutions are the central piece of the acceptance tests platform.

As the exhibit shows, automated staging test solutions rests on automated test workflows and feature defining the test scenarios to ensure digital services meet the customer and business expectations.

Automated Staging Test solutions take advantage of infrastructure as code mechanisms to provision as needed and configure the required resources – servers, networking, storage, and more.

The following table lists some of the top and reliable AST solutions you can invest in:

UAT Tools	Companies	Description
Selenium	Selenium	Selenium is possibly the most popular open-source test automation framework for Web applications. Selenium supports multiple system environments (Windows, Mac, Linux) and browsers (Chrome, Firefox, IE, and Headless browsers). Its scripts can be written in various programming languages such as Java, Groovy, Python, C#, PHP, Ruby, and Perl. While testers have flexibility with Selenium and they can write complex and advanced test scripts to meet various levels of complexity, it requires advanced programming skills and effort to build automation frameworks and libraries for specific testing needs.
Katalon Studio	Katalon	Katalon Studio is a powerful test automation solution for web application, mobile, and web services. Being built on top of the Selenium and Appium frameworks, Katalon Studio takes advantage of these solutions for integrated software automation. The tool supports different levels of testing skill set. Non-programmers can find it easy to start an automation testing project (like using Object Spy to record test scripts) while programmers and advanced automation testers can save time from building new libraries and maintaining their scripts.
Unified Functional Testing (UFT)	Microfocus	UFT is a well-known commercial testing tool for functional testing. It provides a comprehensive feature set for API, web services, and GUI testing of desktop, web, and mobile applications across platforms. The tool has advanced image-based object recognition feature, reusable test components, and automated documentation. UFT uses Visual Basic Scripting Edition to register testing processes and object control. UFT is integrated with Mercury Business Process Testing and Mercury Quality Center. The tool supports CI via integration with CI tools such as Jenkins.

Figure 60 - Top User Acceptance Test (UAT) Tools

Production Technology Stack

Monitoring and tracking digital service business, technological, and technical environment as well as customers' satisfaction is the safest way to make them loyal and keep the company competitive.

That's the objective of the production platform.

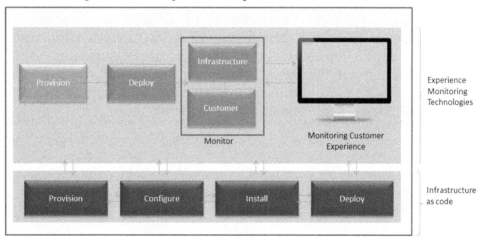

Figure 61 - Production Technology Stack

Customer Experience (CX) Monitoring technologies are the hub of the production platform.

As the exhibit shows, they take advantage of infrastructure as code mechanisms to provision, install and configure as needed the required infrastructure then deploy applications and monitor customer experience.

The following table lists some of the top CX monitoring platforms you can invest in:

CX Management Tools	Companies	Description
Oracle CX Platform	Oracle	The Oracle CX platform is a suite of cloud-based tools that help your business provide a consistent service to your customers. The Oracle CX platform is a suite of cloud-based tools for CRM and sales, marketing, customer service, e-commerce and other tools, such as configure, price quote tools.
IBM CX Suite	IBM	This customer experience software integrates web portal, social and mobile technologies with content and analytics to help you anticipate customer needs and build brand loyalty. Create more targeted, contextual content with a cloud-based solution helping you integrate applications on and off premises for faster deployment at lower cost. Respond to individual expectations, reach more customers and deliver exceptional customer experiences.

Figure 62 - Top CX Management tools you can invest in

What You Must Keep in Mind

The GAFAs' domination and its corollary, the expansion of the network economy and the digital disruptions that go with it, are a reality that you should not approach lightly.

You must rely on proven solutions that have nothing to do with the marketing hypes that proliferate throughout the internet, even when it comes from the major IT brands.

As this chapter demonstrated, the DevOps for Digital Service Development (BlueBird) platform is a proven solution that'll help your business, in record time, take advantage of the digital economy.

Invest in the BlueBird platform to transform your organization's organizational infrastructure and infrastructure, technological infrastructure alone will never make your business competitive.

8. How WellBeing Uses the BlueBird Platform to Grow

At this point in your discovery of the DevOps revolution, you might be thinking, "*Wow! so that's DevOps!*" and trying to convince yourself, you ask, "*So how does this platform work in real life business?*"

This chapter concretely answers this question, it illustrates, step-by-step, how the platform is used, from the changes in the marketplace to product delivery through design and development.

To make sure you get the maximum value out of this chapter, it'll build on what a business day looks like at WellBeing and on how the BlueBird platform is used to deliver innovations that disrupt the diet industry.

Using the BlueBird platform to deliver innovations that disrupt markets is what this chapter is about.

This chapter covers:

- BlueBird is primarily a complete business environment
- Anticipating the next diet industry disruption
- Developing the 4th generation wearable step-by-step

BlueBird is Primarily a Complete Business Environment

This section describes the complete business environment that resulted from the BlueBird platform deployment.

Unlike the traditional notion of platform which stresses and technology and IT tools, the BlueBird platform is primarily a complete work environment.

As illustrated in the second part of the exhibit, it's an agile work environment designed to create positive network effects.

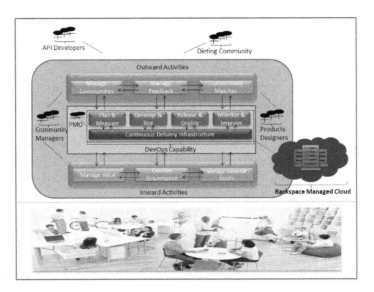

Figure 63 - WellBeing BlueBird-based Business Environment

WellBeing's platform combines two elements fundamental to the company's competitiveness :

- The organizational infrastructure concerned with creating the conditions for positive network effects
- The technological infrastructure concerned with providing the computing power needed to boost the conditions of positive network effects

Let's discuss them.

Agile Organizational Infrastructure Thought to Create and Step Up Positive Network Effects

In WellBeing's digital strategy, the organizational infrastructure is the most importance piece of the business as it provides the fundamental enablers of positive network effects.

Let's see how it works.

Outward Activities

Being aware of the slightest change in the diet market – new competitors, API developers, consumers, and products – and understanding the impacts on the company and triggering the actions to strengthen its network effects is the top priority.

WellBeing builds on three outward activities including:

- Community management

- Feedback management
- Consumate matches

Community Management – is about building, growing, and managing API Developer and consumer communities with the objective of equipping WellBeing with a powerful network effects.

The challenge of the community manager is to guarantee consumers and API developers superior experience with the Activity Tracker features and the provided API development infrastructure.

Feedback Management – is about capturing API Developer and consumer communities feedback and derive from them improvement and innovation ideas.

Inward Activities

Ensuring that activities aimed at creating or strengthening the company's network effects are properly performed and deliver the expected business benefits is another top priority.

WellBeing rests on three inward activities enabled by a DevOps capability. They include:

- Manage value
- Oversee governance
- Manage external assets

Manage value – Seeks to bring in value through several activities including improving API developers and consumers experience and designing and implementing Activity Trackers' new features.

Manage value activities are part of the *Develop & Test* and *Release & Deploy* phases of the company's DevOps capability.

Oversee governance – It's the set of activities concerned with participation in the WellBeing's platform ecosystem, dividing the generated value, and resolving conflicts.

Oversee governance activities are part of the Plan & Measure and Monitor & Improve phases of the company's DevOps capability.

Manage external assets – It's the set of activities concerned with the value derived from the company's external resources including the Rackspace's managed PaaS cloud and other external vendors.

Manage external assets activities are part of the Plan & Measure and Monitor & Improve phases of WellBeing's DevOps capability.

DevOps Capability

Relying on a software delivery culture that's not only stress speed but also fosters innovation, operational and organizational agility and its corollary, responsiveness to market opportunities, is the hub of the company's digital strategy.

WellBeing's DevOps capability provides the cultural elements – innovation and collaborative mindset, focus on customer value – that unlock the company's responsiveness and make a major disruptor of the diet market.

Rackspace Managed-PaaS Cloud Designed to Get Rid of the Hassles of Managing IT and Guarantee Positive Customer Experience

WellBeing's digital strategy is unimaginable without the technology platform that makes its technological infrastructure.

It's implemented as a managed-cloud infrastructure designed to cut IT costs and allow low prices and make IT operations faster and accelerate time-to-market and time-to-revenue.

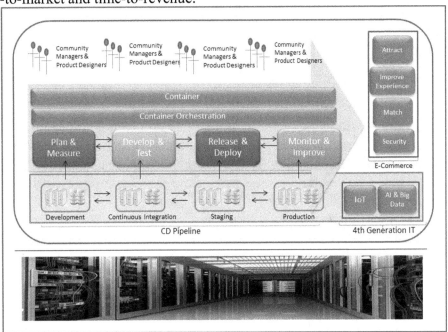

Figure 64 - WellBeing Technological Infrastructure

WellBeing's technological infrastructure combines three platforms including:

- The continuous delivery (CD) pipeline
- The E-Commerce platform

- And what they call the Fourth Generation technologies

Let's discuss them.

The Central Role of the CD Pipeline

Hosted in a Rackspace managed PaaS cloud which is built on Google GAE, the CD pipeline, the *Toolchain* as they call it, is the hub of the company's Activity Trackers development effort; it automates the end-to-end product development process.

It's a four-step traditional continuous delivery pipeline augmented with what the company's CIO name our fourth generation technologies – Internet of Things (IoT) and Big Data Analytics.

Through orchestrating as one release workflow the continuous integration, test, and deployment phases, WellBeing's CD pipeline implements the continuous paradigm.

How The E-Commerce Infrastructure Enables The Platform Model

WellBeing's platform seeks to put together a community of Activity Tracker consumers and API developers and take advantage of that community to continuously increase consumers value – the money spent to consume the company's service.

The underpinning logic is, the more loyal consumers, the bigger consumer, and the wealthier the company.

The E-commerce as they call it, perform three primary functions to intensify interactions and create positive network effects, these functions include:

- Attract
- Improve Experience
- Match

Attract – As the name suggests, this function attracts API developers, partners, and consumers to put them into a community and intensify interactions to create positive network effects.

It builds on two strategic activities including *Content Marketing* and *Customer Relationships Management (CRM)*.

Content Marketing by creating and sharing online material (videos, blogs, social media posts) implicitly stimulates interests in WellBeing's activity trackers.

CRM by allowing WellBeing to manage relationships and the data and information associated with API developers, partners, and consumers.

It plays a central role in keeping API developers, partners, ans consumers loyal to the platform.

Improve Experience – As suggested, this function facilitate the interactions between API developers, partners, and consumers in an effort to offer a superior customer experience and creative highly positive network effects.

It builds on *Collaborative and Sharing* technology and takes advantage of *Big Data Analytics* tools to continuously analyze feedback, measure API developers, partners, and activity tracker users satisfaction, and implement improvements.

Match – As suggested, this function matches three things, the first is, the activity tracker consumers with the right partner services, the second is the API developers with the right partner services, and last is, the activity tracker users with the API developers concerned with their product features.

Anticipating the Next Diet Industry Disruption

Let's understand the competitive context first!

How the Obamacare Disrupted the Industry

The Obamacare's prevention policy was disrupting the healthcare and wellness industries; it favored techie gadgets and the do-it-yourself approaches.

The changes it brought in healthcare was resulting in far more consumer-centric products; technology breakthroughs and the increasing adoption of mobile devices offered profit opportunities.

How Fitbit Initiative Disrupted the Market

The demand for wearables were also gaining traction; something like 45 percent of Americans were interested in wearable devices, and about 10 percent already used trackers, such as the $100 Fitbit Flex.

As a matter of fact, Fitbit, launched seven years ago, covers 69 percent of the market followed by the Jawbone brand at 14 percent.

Over the holidays, Fitbit started a first TV campaign on network and cable in the U.S. as well as in Asia Pacific and Europe; it shows athletic people running, rock climbing, rowing and biking with a mantra of *"bikefit, paddlefit, gracefit and holy fit,"* Campaign Us' Joan Voight put it in a remarkable article.

The messsage was designed to show that fitness was different for everyone, according to the company. The ads was backed by digital and cinema.

Why WellBeing Had to React?

Industry analysts all agree on one thing, this was a promising first step. Wearables cloud reach everyday consumers only if they keep it simple.

"The brand should provide easy ways to let people learn about how it works and connect with them using other high-value touch points, such as an app that encourages them to use the device or an event where wearables are common," Joan Voight reported.

Industry's players should also understand that mass-market, low-tech consumers are not looking for another device that operates on its own. *"They want something that seamlessly fits into other products that have made their way into their lives,"* she said.

That's how, equipped with thes BlueBird platform, WellBeing decided to counter-attack with a new generation of wearables.

Developing The 4ᵗʰ Generation Wearable Step-by-Step

The following exhibit represents the workflow supporting, across the company, the design, development, testing, and deployment of the fourth generation wearables:

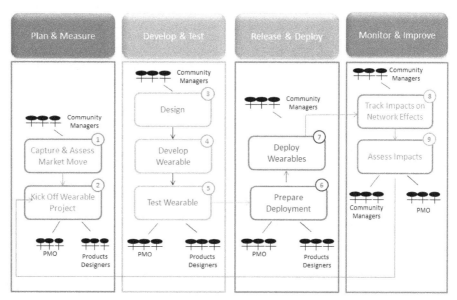

Figure 65 - WellBeing DevOps Lifecycle

The community managers; product designers, and the PMO are mobilized throughout the DevOps lifecycle to make sure objectives are achieved.

Let's how each step of the process is performed from the staff, methodology, tools and technology perspectives.

Plan & Measure

This step of the DevOps lifecycle was focused on monitoring the changes in the diet market. Two primary executive tasks was performed – *Capture & Assess Market Moves and Kick Off Wearable Project.*

Capture & Assess Market Moves

Capture & Assess Market Moves is triggered everytime something happens in the diet industry – new competitors, new products, merger & acquisition, partnerships – likely to affect the company's network effects.

The bottom is to responsively spot the threats, assess the impacts on the company, and decide on the proper reactions.

As part of WellBeing's outward activities, *Capture & Assess Market Moves* mobilizes, the community managers, product designers and the PMO to collect market data and information to perform industry analyses.

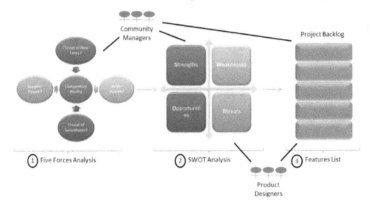

Figure 66 - WellBeing's Market Monitoring Activity Diagram

Five Forces Analysis, *SWOT analysis*, and *Scrum Agile Product Backlog* methodologies and related tools – *Cipher Competitive Analysis Toolkit* and and *JIRA Agile* – are used to investigate the diet market changes.

Kick Off Wearable Project

Kick Off Wearable Project is triggered to instantiate the predefined and standardized DevOps capability – staff, structure, methodology, and tools – that will support the company's reaction to market events.

The bottom line is to responsively set up a project structure that'll take on the company's challenge.

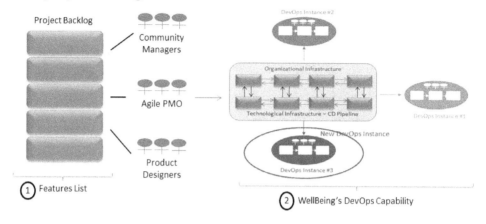

Figure 67 - WellBeing's Project Kick Off Activity Diagram

As illustrated, *Kick Off Wearable Project* is part of WellBeing's inward activities, it mobilizes community managers, product designers, and more importantly, the Agile PMO set up, custodian of WellBeing's DevOps culture, set up the change project and kick it off.

The most important point here is, how the notion of DevOps-style project instance is used to kick off change projects. A predefined scrum agile project chart is used, it primarily clarifies the team structure and the project timeline.

The team structure includes a designated Agile PMO acting as the *Scrum Master*, a designated community manager acting as the *Product Owner*, and members of the company's product designers acting as development team members.

Product Backlog and *Sprint Backlog* are used to the project's overall effort while a *Burn Down Chart* is used to track progress.

Develop & Test

This stage is the hub of the company's value chain; it's where innovative ideas are validated, translated into product ideas and then implemented.

Three activities make it up – *Design Wearable*, *Develop Wearable*, and *Test Wearable*.

Design Wearable

Design Wearable is started once the DevOps instance supporting the company's new challenge is started.

The stake here is to design activity tracker features that solve consumer problems, and strengthen or create powerful network effects.

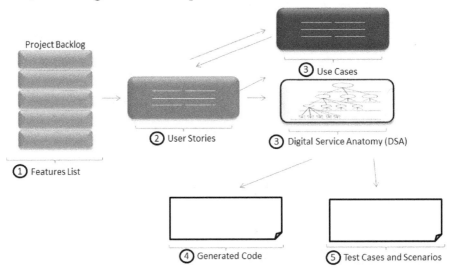

Figure 68 - WellBeing Develop and Test Diagram Activity

As part of WellBeing's inward activities, *Design Wearable* mobilizes the DevOps instance's community manager, product designer, and the development team to define the features of the expected solution and then design or update the activity tracker's design.

A combination of methodologies and tools are leveraged and integrated into an *Activity Tracker Design* process.

The *User Story Map* and *Use Case Diagram* are used to collect the agreed upon solutions, categorize them and map them to the DSA as primary and secondary functions.

The corresponding source code and test cases and scenarios are generated from the DSA model to accelerate activity trackers' development.

Develop Wearable

Develop Wearable is triggered when the activity tracker design is stable and, more importantly, actionable.

The challenge is to concretely implement activity tracker features in line with the expectations and recommendations agreed upon in the design phase.

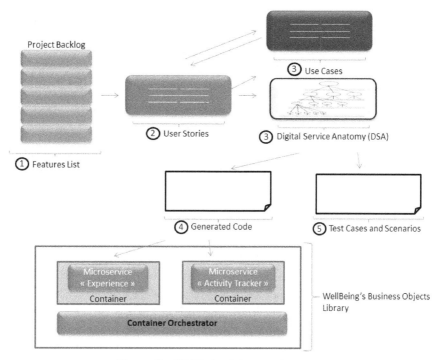

Figure 69 - WellBeing Microservices Approach

As part of WellBeing's inward activities, *Develop Wearable* involves community manager, product designers, and the development team to implement activity tracker's features.

A development approach combining Microservices and Docker containers is used to accelerate the delivery.

What they do is, they use containers as the portable code envelope and decompose applications into many Microservices that are independently built and deployed.

The company's DevOps culture by fostering accelerated integrations, extensive interactions between the community manager, the product designer, and the development team not to mention the CD pipeline that speeds up the overall effort, plays a key role in WellBeing's competitiveness.

Test Wearable

Testing is started very early in the *Develop Wearable* phase; the objective is to proactively identify and remove bugs and dysfunctional behaviors in a way that guarantees accelerated time-to-market and time-to-revenue.

As part of WellBeing's inward activities, *Test Wearable* mobilizes community manager, product designers, and the development team to test activity tracker's features.

To guarantee superior customer experience while ensuring effectiveness and productivity three testing approaches are used including *Continuous Quality Assurance (QA)*, *User Acceptance Test (UAT) Automation*, and , and *Operational Acceptance Test (OAT) Automation*.

Continuous QA – In WellBeing's application containerization context, the principle is to perform parallel modular testing using Test-Driven Development (TDD) and Behavior-Driven Development (BDD).

They're enabled by automation through continuous unit test and sandbox testing at the Microservice level. Testing early and often to proactively identify diagnose and fix errors using automation is vital for the company.

UAT Automation – To reduce error risks to the maximum and secure deployment to production, user acceptance test are automated.

OAT Automation – To eradicate as much as possible issues that damage customer experience like device poor responsiveness, OAT are automated.

The objective is to evaluate the performance impact on the customer experience.

Release & Deploy

This third stage is focused on preparing the digital product's launch and deploy it onto the market.

Two primary activities compose it including *Prepare Deployment* and *Deploy Wearable*.

Prepare Deployment

Prepare Deployment is proactively triggered during the activity tracker features implementation.

The bottom line is to create conditions for a powerful sales momentum as well as powerful network effects.

As part of WellBeing's inward activities, *Prepare Deployment* mobilizes community manager, Agile PMO, product designer, and the development team to discuss the activity tracker's launch plan.

In the prepping meeting the following issues are discussed:

- Deployment timeline
- Deployment channels including social medias
- Content marketing supporting activity tracker launch

- Activity tracker's functional and technical readiness

Deploy Wearable

Deploy Wearable is automatically triggered to once activity trackers have been tested and experimented.

The objective is to introduce new features in the market. As part of WellBeing's outward activities, *Deploy Wearable* mobilizes community manager, product designer, and the development team to monitor the automated deployment of the activity tracker onto the market.

Monitor & Improve

The primary purpose of this last stage is to monitor and continuously improve the API developers and consumers experience with the activity trackers.

Two activities make it up including *Track Impacts on Network Effects* and *Assess Impacts*.

Track and Assess Impacts on Network Effects

Track Impacts on Network Effects is performed on 24/7 basis to track consumers' satisfactions with the activity tracker features and API developers satisfaction with the platform provided to help them do their job.

As part of WellBeing's outward activities, *Track Impacts on Network Effects* involves primarily the community manager assisted by product designers and IT operations members of the development team.

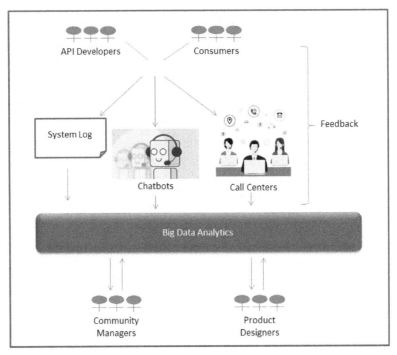

Figure 70 - WellBeing Feedback Tracking System

As illustrated, to track feedback data, WellBeing leverages a combination of techniques and technologies including system logs analysis, chatbots, and call center.

Chatbots are artificial intelligence (AI) software that simulates a conversation with a user in natural language through messaging applications, websites, mobile apps or through the telephone.

Big Data analytics are used to turn data into actionable consumer, product, and market information.

What You Must Keep in Mind

You've probably noticed it, unlike many of its competitors which went the opposite direction, WellBeing like the GAFAs, equipped itself with three fundamental things:

- A digital business strategy
- A platform business model
- The BlueBird platform as its DevOps capability

Don't get trapped by the massive hypes suggesting that implementing DevOps is about about implementing CD infrastructure, and that implementing technology is all you need to succeed.

Rather, remember that DevOps is a two-dimension capability – organizational and technological – and we need both, one cannot go without the other.

The GAFAs took the business world into a new paradigm, the *Network Economy*, transforming the entire business, ***not only*** the IT infrastructure, is the way to go.

9. The Future of DevOps

Despite its unexplored potential which transcends IT issues, DevOps seems to confine itself to software deployment and IT operations concerns.

That would be bad because, its approach offers the elements IT needs to help businesses survive and thrive in the rising network economy.

Combining approaches such as Agile, Lean, and continuous deployment into a software deployment culture for innovation, responsiveness, and competitiveness is a genius idea.

Gene Kim, Kevin Behr, George Spafford, Jez Humble, Patrick Debois, John Willis, and John Allspaw in "*The Phoenix Project*" and "*The DevOps Handbook,*" laid the foundation of the ongoing IT revolution.

The future of IT isn't in the blind deployment of the latest technology innovations; it's in the ability of the IT community to understand the changes in the competitive environment and supply not only tools and infrastructure but also to help businesses transform.

Without these transformations, expecting revenue and competitiveness is pure wishful thinking.

This chapter covers:

- Going beyond IT's productivity thinking
- Additional assets are needed to meet digital challenges
- Disrupting the status quo imposed by certain vendors and CIOs
- Adopting DevOps' two-component vision is the future

Going Beyond IT's Productivity Thinking

Productivity – producing more, cheaper, faster and with less means – is no longer a competitive advantage.

Technology, particularly information technology (IT), which has long been the primary productivity driver, is no longer, the unique competitiveness factor.

Facts speak for themselves, Nine West Holdings, The Bon-Ton Stores, Toys R Us, Remington, Southeastern Grocers, Tops Markets, Sears, they all invested either in Cloud Computing, or in DevOps and for some of them in both. They all went bankrupt.

It's urgent for IT to reinvent itself and build on a paradigm that goes beyond IT tools concerns.

Additional Assets are Needed to Meet Digital Challenges

My point isn't that IT doesn't matter anymore, IT will continue to matter as long as productivity will remain one of the key drivers of value.

Competitive environments have changed, productivity, therefore IT isn't anymore enough to generate revenue; businesses are increasingly dealing with proliferating competitors.

Additional assets are needed including innovation, responsiveness, operational agility, and collaborative mindset.

Without these competitive advantages that I grouped together under the concept of *organizational infrastructure*, chances are thousands of businesses go bankrupt and millions of workers around the globe loose their job.

DevOps' Two-Component Vision is the Future

As weird as it might seem, DevOps is the only IT approach that addresses the non-technological competitive advantages.

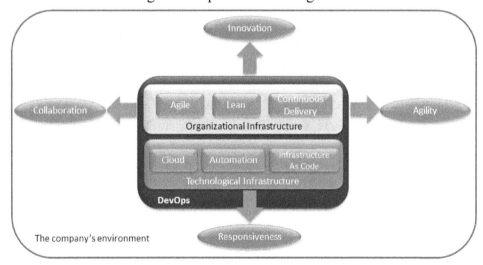

Figure 71 - DevOps as the competitive advantages' enabler

As illustrated, DevOps sees the company as a two-component entity including the well-known technological infrastructure and the widely ignored organizational infrastructure.

The fact of the matter is, DevOps acts as an enabler of the competitive edges needed to survive and thrive in the network economy.

What I'd like you to be aware of is, the organizational infrastructure by leveraging the Agile, Lean and Continuous Delivery approaches, enables three vital competitive advantages: innovation, collaborative, and responsiveness mindsets.

Will DevOps Survive?

The question is worth asking, will DevOps survive?

In the early 2000s, the Project Management Office (PMO) concept created the same hopes and enthusiasm as DevOps. It was rightly presented as the approach that would finally bring IT closer to business concerns and priorities.

In three years, the concept of PMO and its promises were reduced to dust by the major IT vendors, they narrowed it to reporting and dashboarding tools.

The same thing is repeating with DevOps, the IT community is imposing the erroneous idea that the so-called DevOps tools by themselves will provide business lines with the competitiveness they're desperately looking for.

I reiterate my point: That's not true!

What You Must Keep in Mind

To conclude, I cite Harvard's Professor Michael Porter, one of the brightest mind in competitive strategy, what he thinks about today's capitalism is indicative of what could happen to DevOps.

He argues, *"The capitalist system is under siege. In recent years business has been criticized as a major cause of social, environmental, and economic problems. Companies are widely thought to be prospering at the expense of their communities. Trust in business has fallen to new lows, leading government officials to set policies that undermine competitiveness and sap economic growth. Business is caught in a vicious circle."*

Then concludes, *"A big part of the problem lies with companies themselves, which remain trapped in an outdated, narrow approach to value creation. Focused on optimizing short-term financial performance, they overlook the greatest unmet needs in the market as well as broader influences on their long-term success. Why else would companies ignore the well-being of their customers, the depletion of natural resources vital to their businesses, the viability of suppliers, and the economic distress of the communities in which they produce and sell?."*

Apply the principles and recommendations of this book, they guarantee tangible business benefits.

Let's make the DevOps revolution, let's disrupt the status quo, let's shift today's IT thinking from IT modernization concern to digital competitiveness and revenue priority.

10. Going Further With The DevOps Revolution

Most training, online courses and webinars on the recent technology innovations stress the tool dimension and claim, *"On their own, IT tools create business value."* As demonstrated throughout this book, that statement isn't true. Many articles, testimonies, case studies, and surveys show the growing frustration of businesses.

What many IT executives don't understand is, these recent technology innovations are disruptive; implementing them to boost business benefits demands a deep transformation of the company.

The cloud for example, by ridding the company of managing IT, doesn't only reduce costs and speed up IT operations, it also offers the unprecedented opportunity to make the business interactions agile, flexible, and responsive to markets. The fact of the matter is, these interactions are achieved by proactively transform the company, by adjusting the way it does business.

Very few businesss and IT leaders are aware of it; they think the transformation will automatically take place right after IT implementation.

The same reasoning applies to DevOps, focusing on the tool aspect modernizes the IT infrastructure, with unfortunately very few impacts on the business benefits.

The secret of successful digital transformation is, the concerned business and IT leaders understood the whys and wherefores of digital disruption, they understood that, deploying IT in an effort to make the business competitive demands the transformation of two fundamental things of the company: the technological infrastructure and the organizational infrastructure.

That's why some savvy experts talk about the cloud and DevOps as disruptive technologies; they demand a transformation of the business.

The Digital IT Academy, founded and led by Philippe Abdoulaye, offers online courses, presentations, and workshops around digital transformation based on cloud computing and DevOps.

This chapter discusses the recommended courses that follow:

- The complete guide for taking your business digital

- How to yield business benefits with DevOps Now™
- Transform your business with Enterprise Cloud Now™

The Complete Guide for Taking Your Business Digital

This online course is the practical guide to leading all aspects – strategic, organizational, and technological – of your business digital transformation.

This two-hour and fifteen-module course addresses the following topics:

- The key things to know about your industry's disruption
- Innovation is the foundation of the digital survival and success
- The secret for continuous innovation: optimize your value stream
- DevOps is the foundation your digital organization's operations
- Your digital transformation journey: the key success factors
- Clarify your innovation strategy using the IVC™
- Leading your DevOps capability design
- Leading your CD Infrastructure (CDI) design
- The implementation phase overview
- Facilitating the value stream implementation
- Facilitating the CDI implementation
- Managing the pilot experiment project
- Deploying the organizational changes
- Where to go from this course

The course is widely adopted in Asia particularly in Hong-Kong, Singapore, and Indonesia where sales are boosting as unexpected.

The following sections give an overview of the fifteen modules that make up this unprecedented presentation on implementing DevOps to turn a business digital.

The Key Things to Know About Your Industry's Digital Disruption

This first module defines digital disruption and tells the impacts on your business and on the IT organization.

 The Key Things to Know about Your Industry's Disruption

- The unknown industry disruption drivers

- Case study - How Toy R Us was forced out of business

The following questions are answered:

- What is digital disruption?
- What are its core drivers?
- How does it affect your company's model?
- Why you need to pay attention to it?

How Amazon disrupted the toy retail market and force Toys R Us out of business is cited by companies who attended the course as the "climax" part of the module:

 #1 The Key Things to Know about Your Industry's Disruption

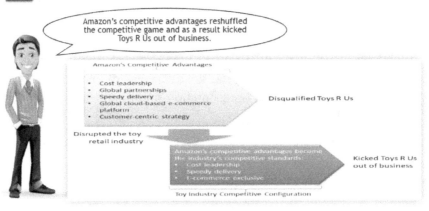

You'll learn about Amazon's competitive advantages that disrupted the toy retail industry.

Innovation is the Foundation of Your Digital Survival and Success

This module provides a realistic perspective of innovation and tells what business lines of top five hundreds companies mean by innovation.

#2 Innovation is the Foundation of Your Digital Survival and Success

● Innovation is your primary value driver
● Why successful businesses rely on well-thought innovation strategies
● Develop your innovation strategy step-by-step with the Innovation Virtuous Circle (IVC™)

The module answers key questions including:

- How innovation and sophistication differ?
- What business lines have in mind when they talk about innovation?
- What's the *Innovation Virtuous Circle (IVC™)*? Why does it matter?

How innovation capability design workshops are led including the agenda, the processes, the tools and mobilized staff is cited by most companies as the most exciting moment of this module:

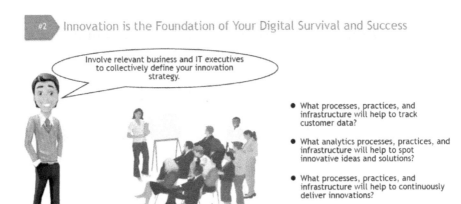

You and your team will learn the whys and wherefores of implementing enterprise innovation capabilities.

The Secret for Continuous Innovation: Optimize Your Organization's Value Chain

This module puts the finger where it hurts: business value is created in your company's value stream, technology is just a very powerful enabler of business value.

This third module answers the following question:

- What's the value stream? Where does this notion come from?
- What's the connection with the concept of value chain?
- What's meant by optimizing your organization's value chain?

The structure and how the value stream impacts your organization ability to deliver business value is cited by most companies as the "top moment" of this module:

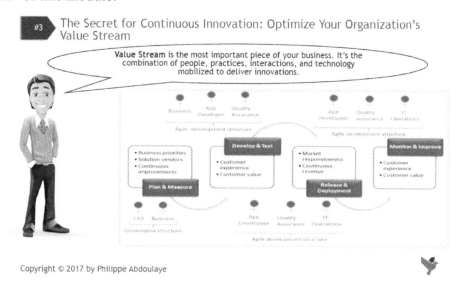

You'll learn a very demanded skill in today's business: value stream optimizations.

Your Digital Transformation Journey: Clarify Your Innovation Strategy Using the IVC™

This module discusses the very strategic issue of the digital transformation journey. A powerful risk-oriented digital transformation tool that's been helping hundreds of companies around the world.

The following issues are addressed:

- What's a digital transformation journey? What's its structure? How does it work?
- How does it help to optimize companies' value streams?
- How does it help to implement DevOps CD infrastructure?

Defining the digital and innovation strategy is praised by most companies as a very important moment in this central module:

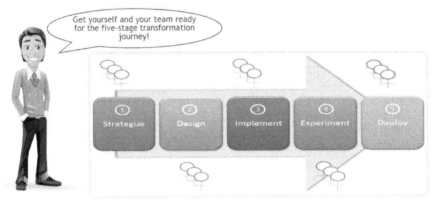

You'll get insights into the unknown and misunderstood world of digital transformation including actionable methodologies, techniques, and tools in the areas of:

- Organizational and operational transformation
- DevOps CD infrastructure implementation
- DevOps culture deployment and adoption
- And more

It's impossible to cover everything you need to know about this very successful online course on digital transformation, that'll be too long.

Visit the Digital IT Academy to explore the course's curriculum and know more. It's at: https://digital-it-academy.teachable.com/

Transform Your Business with Enterprise Cloud Now™

This online course is the practical guide to leading all aspects of Enterprise Cloud transformation.

This one-hour and seven-module online presentation discusses the following issues:

- The good to know about enterprise cloud and cloud computing
- Challenges and weaknesses you didn't know about today's cloud implementation approach
- What's Enterprise Cloud (EC)? What's make it specific?
- Why investing in EC will durably boost your digital business?
- The key steps to take for migrating a business to EC?
- Enteprise cloud migration: the step-by-step journey
- Where to go from here?

The course is widely taught in Asia particularly in Hong-Kong, Singapore, and Indonesia where sales are boosting as unexpected.

The following sections give an overview of the seven modules that make it up.

Weaknesses and Challenges You Didn't Know About Today's Cloud Approaches

This module discusses the weaknesses and challenges of today's cloud computing implementation approaches.

It unveils the reasons why cloud migration projects, so far, do not deliver the value expected by business lines.

#1 Weaknesses and Challenges You Didn't Know About Today's Cloud Approaches

- The ignored industry disruption challenges
- Cloud computing isn't used at its full potential
- The challenge is to fix the impacts on the business and on the IT organization

The following topics are addressed:

- The ignored industry disruption challenges
- Why cloud computing isn't used as its full potential
- Why fixing industry disruption impacts on the business and IT is the challenge

Clarifying the industry disruption factors affecting the business competitiveness is cited by most companies as the top moment of this module:

#1.2 Defining Digital Disruption and the Impacts on the Business

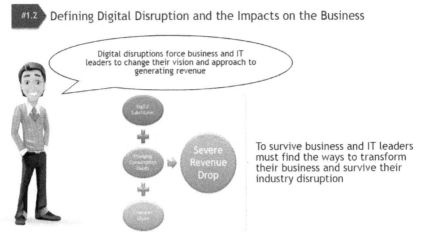

Digital disruptions force business and IT leaders to change their vision and approach to generating revenue

Severe Revenue Drop

To survive business and IT leaders must find the ways to transform their business and survive their industry disruption

You well get insights into how digital technologies disrupt industry and force businesses to transform entirely, not only the IT infrastructure.

Enterprise Cloud Migration: The Step-by-Step Journey

This module addresses the very strategic enterprise cloud transformation journey. Without it cloud migration projects result in organizational messes.

The following questions are answered:
- How to develop a digital business strategy based on cloud computing?
- How to design, end-to-end, an enterprise cloud architecture? How to select the right cloud technologies and service providers?
- What's an enterprise cloud migration plan? How to develop it?
- How to migrate business and datacenter functions to cloud computing?

Exploring in detail the five steps of the enterprise cloud migration journey from the staff, process, best practice, methodology, and tool perspective is cited by most companies as the top moment of the module:

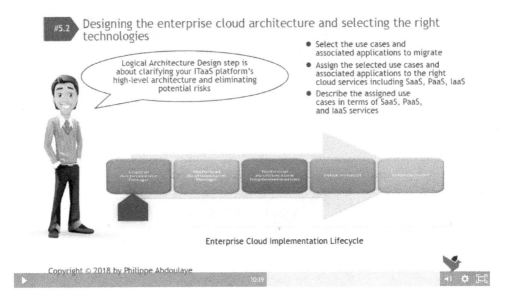

You'll get insights into how to design a logical and technical enterprise cloud architecture, how to implement it, experiment it through a pilot project, and deploy it.

You'll learn how to leverage simple tools, yet as vital as, the enterprise cloud design matrices:

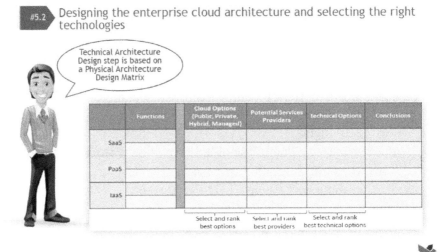

These are collaborative tools that simplifies and accelerates enterprise cloud engineering tasks.

It's impossible to cover everything you need to know about this very successful online course on digital transformation, that'll be too long.

Visit the Digital IT Academy to explore the course's curriculum and know more. It's at: https://digital-it-academy.teachable.com/

Appendix A – Is Today's DevOps The Next Fiasco

Published on DevOps.com in 2018, this article went viral and was praised by many observers of the IT industry as challenging to today's DevOps deployment practice.

....

I chose to share the findings of a TechRepublic's recent survey on DevOps not only because it's a bombshell within the IT community, but because it brings out two eye-opening facts:

1. Seventy-eight percent of organizations haven't fully implemented DevOps because "they don't get it"
2. Only 22 percent of organizations have merged their teams for managing infrastructure, operations and development

In other words, the message underneath is, "*You must consider most DevOps success stories with a pinch of salt.*"

The big question is, Why are all these DevOps implementation failures happening? That's where I bring the answers most experts, including renowned thought leaders, for some reason won't give you.

The findings of this vital survey shouldn't leave you indifferent. Your company's survival and growth depend on them. They're recurrently raised in all the conferences and workshops I give. "*We deployed the automation toolchain; honestly, I don't see the business value,*" or "*Making the business, development, testing and operations work together is an impossible challenge,*" is all I hear all the time. The last time I had to address these complaints was at the Econocom's DevOps Seminar in Toulouse, France.

The answers I provide result in the same reactions: Companies successfully change their DevOps vision and implementation approach.

Believe it or not, that's my six-year experience advising on DevOps worldwide, as well as the observations of an increasing number of reliable IT industry analysts including Joe McKendrick and Jason Bloomberg. The three fundamental failure factors of DevOps implementation are:

1. Either a lack of or unclear business objectives.
2. Widespread misconceptions of DevOps including among thought leaders.
3. Conflicting interests of the DevOps tools business.

Let me give you a few ideas that will either help you monetize your organization's transition to DevOps or adjust your existing DevOps capability and make it profitable.

Unclear Business Objectives Result in Irrelevant DevOps Capabilities

Again, that's my experience and the observations of many IT industry analysts, most DevOps initiatives are disconnected from any business objectives.

In all the workshops I conduct, the question, *"What's your business goal?"* gets the same blurry answers: *"Adopting DevOps is a must,"* *"We must automate our IT processes,"* *"Making our IT agile will make our business competitive,"* *"Speeding up delivery is a competitive advantage our business lines will like,"* and *"Automating our IT processes will do good to the business."*

What you must know is, these goals range from vague and fake to inappropriate and nonexistent. They primarily serve the IT department's interests. Not the business.

The fact is, there's a significant gap between business line expectations and the DevOps benefits as imagined by your IT leader peers and their associated vendors. The business looks to meet the challenges of the disrupted markets created by Google, Amazon, Facebook and Apple (GAFA, in the rest of the article)—competition which includes continuous innovation, accelerated time-to-revenue, cost reduction, low prices and market responsiveness. And the only help DevOps experts offer is the acceleration of applications delivery and the automation of IT operations. Is it enough? The answer is clearly no; it's a drop in the ocean.

The GAFA are disrupting your company's markets. The only chance to resist them is to adjust your business model to the new competitive constraints. Because they didn't transform as their disrupted markets required, Nine West Holdings, the Bon-Ton Stores, Toys R Us, Remington, Southeastern Grocers and Tops Markets were all kicked out of business. Read what Business Insider's Hailey Peterson said about it in a recent article.

I encourage you to involve your business lines in your DevOps project and agree with them on a clear business objective. Then, implement DevOps to enable that objective. Otherwise, that's wasted time and more importantly, wasted investment!

The Secret of DevOps Has Always Been About How Well You Work, not Technology

This is something I hope you won't doubt: Most experts including renowned thought leaders play on words to present DevOps as close to either an agile software development framework or a continuous delivery infrastructure (CDI).

Let's say it straight: That vision, now adopted by CIOs, is erroneous and has been taking thousands of businesses into the wall.

Adam Jacob's article, **The Secret of DevOps, It's Always Been About People, Not Technology,** provides from my perspective, the best definition of DevOps. It presents it primarily as, "... *fundamentally about taking the behaviors and beliefs that draw us together as people, combining them with a deep understanding of our customers' needs, and using that knowledge to ship better products to our customers.*" But he makes it clear, "*Tools matter. Make no mistake, trying to change the way you work without changing the mechanisms by which you do that work is a futile exercise in excruciating failure. But tools exist in service of the prime directive: building highly functioning, highly effective cross-functional teams, that attack your thorniest business problems as a unit, rather than as lone individuals or silos with competing incentives.*"

What's interesting with Jacob's big picture is, it's definitely business-oriented and takes into account value creation drivers such as the human factor, values and behaviors, processes and practices, cross-functional collaboration and, of course, technology. Every qualified IT leader should understand these drivers as the fundamentals of their company's survival and growth.

So, shrinking DevOps to agile software development and Jenkins, Puppet and Docker, and thinking it will result in revenue doesn't make sense. That's the reason why the 78 percent of organizations in the TechRepublic's survey failed!

Would you agree that to set up a profitable business, the most important thing is to deploy Jenkins, Chef, Docker? I hope not!

DevOps is about how well you mobilize your company's assets— staff and skills, values and behaviors, processes and practices, tools and infrastructure—to make it competitive and wealthy. Adopting DevOps, particularly in today's disrupted industry context, is primarily a business transformation effort. Nothing else!

If you don't want to be part of the 88 percent of organizations that proved unable to merge their team for managing infrastructure, operations and development, like Adam Jacob's article suggests it, tackle DevOps primarily as an agile business operational model. Otherwise, get ready to be among the next GAFA victims!

Preventing the Next DevOps Fiasco

I'm afraid the conditions for the next DevOps fiasco are in place. They have a name: The incredible power of IT vendors.

The incredible power of IT vendors relates to what Harvard's strategist Michael Porter calls the "bargaining power of suppliers." It's the market or industry configuration where the domination of one company or a group of companies reaches a point where they can impose their views, products and services. IT vendors are exactly in that situation.

IT tools have improved productivity so much over the last 30 years that companies have come to believe that they can fix every business problem including innovation, agility and profitability. IT vendors, using massive marketing hypes, are taking advantage of the situation to make millions of dollars. Dollars aren't the problem; it's the poor ROI their clients get.

Will this TechRepublic's survey help to prevent the next DevOps fiasco? Time will tell.

Key Takeaways

Your company's priority is to survive the disrupted markets created by the GAFA. You won't make it happen unless you definitely acknowledge that revenue, the essence of your business, is created as part of complex process that mobilizes across your company's value chain, your staff and skills, values and behaviors, processes and practices and, of course, tools and infrastructure.

If DevOps can't help businesses with what matters right now—survive their industry disruptions— it's definitely useless!

As Chris Tozzi, suggests it, *"The other main possibility for the post-DevOps world is that we'll see DevOps extended into more and more parts of the business that are not directly related to the two core areas of DevOps practice, development and operations."*

Here's a resource that tells you all about how to implement DevOps as the catalyst of your business competitiveness: How to Yield Business Benefits with DevOps.

Appendix B – Why Taking DevOps to the Next Level is Urgent

Published on DevOps.com in 2018, this article went viral and was praised by many observers of the IT industry as challenging to today's DevOps deployment practice.

....

On March 15, I gave four keynote speeches on DevOps in Toulouse, France. As the main speaker of Econocom Club MEP 2018, an annual think tank summit organized by the European business-to-business digital services provider, I shared the day with 15 firms in industries as prestigious as financial services, energy, aerospace, aviation, and telecommunications and heard all about their implementation projects.

The lessons learned from this year's summit are troubling, they tell a story the vast majority of DevOps vendors aren't prepared to hear: They miss their client expectations. There's a severe disconnect between what's expected and what's delivered.

Participant visions and approaches didn't surprise me; they simply confirmed my point that DevOps is misunderstood. By stressing the implementation of Continuous Delivery (CD) toolchains—selling technology is more lucrative than transforming a business—IT service providers aren't helping.

What do these lessons tell, exactly? if you're an open-minded leader who understands that a new IT service delivery paradigm more focused on business concerns is needed, this is for you.

The Untold Frustration

In his opening speech, facilitator Fabrice Berne was inspired to ask participants while they introduced themselves to share the purpose and challenges of their DevOps implementation project.

What I heard didn't surprise me; it was a mix of fascination and frustration—participants were at the same time excited to work on a DevOps project and frustrated because they weren't getting the promised business benefits.

"The reason is, you all tackled your DevOps project the wrong way," I said. *"You started by implementing the CD toolchain, thinking tools on their*

own will deliver the expected business benefits. That illusion is widespread in the IT community!"

So, What is DevOps?

As my claim turned the atmosphere icy, I added, *"DevOps can't be narrowed to these tools—not even to agile practices and automation. It's more than that. DevOps seeks to make the business competitive, wealthy and healthy by continuously delivering high-quality software."* And concluding my introduction, I made it clear: *"The fundamental question is, How is business value created? Many experts, particularly techies, struggle to answer it."*

"Let me say this straight: Most DevOps projects fail because certain experts erroneously spread the idea that the most important piece of DevOps is the CD infrastructure," I said, adding, *"The fact of the matter is these experts and the IT solution vendors they represent are creating confusion; through massive marketing hypes they force CIOs to address DevOps through the distorted lenses of the so-called DevOps tools."*

The Inconsistent Disparate Visions

The following chart results from a survey we conducted at ITaaSNow last year. It involved 2,681 businesses that were unhappy with their cloud and DevOps migration projects; we wanted to show how poor DevOps approaches lead businesses to failure:

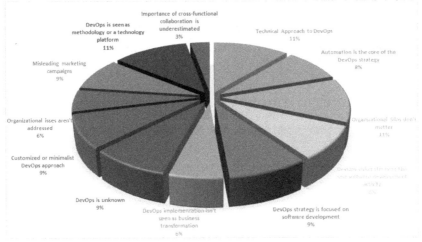

Figure 72 - Disparate and erroneous visions that cause implementation failure

"As you can see, there's no homogeneous perspective right now," I told the audience. *"It varies according to the business culture, objective and strategy or the DevOps architect's understanding, experience and expertise. In most cases, these customized visions are incomplete and generate no business value at all."*

I picked two failure causes in the chart to demonstrate my point.

Starting with the notion that, *"automation is the core of DevOps,"* I argued, *"DevOps primarily seeks to help generate business value. Generating business value is about identifying market and customer expectations, translating expectations into profitable service ideas, developing, deploying, promoting, selling them and continuously improving customer experience."*

"Where did techies get the idea that to make a business profitable the only thing to do is to implement Git, Jenkins, Cucumber and Chef into a CD toolchain?" I asked, somewhat ironically.

Picking a second cause, *"DevOps strategy should only stress software development activity,"* I continued. *"Thinking that isolatedly software development activities will generate business benefits without involving marketing, sales, testing and operations is a pure illusion. Once again, generating business value is a complex process that covers identifying market and customer expectations, translating expectations into profitable service ideas, developing, deploying, promoting, selling them, and continuously improving customer experience."*

"Where did solution vendors get the belief that, software development alone is enough to generate business value?," I asked. *"That's another myth they nurture!"*

I then warned: *"Make no mistake about it: All the visions represented on the chart are either incomplete or wrong. They do not reflect what DevOps is. You must acknowledge once and for all that it's a business transformation effort, not only an IT capability implementation. Period."*

The Contrast with the Founding Fathers' Vision

"Who better than its founders can provide the right vision and definition of DevOps?" I asked.

Relying on Jesse Robins, John Allspaw and Paul Hammond's vision as reported by Chef co-founder Adam Jacob in a memorable article, "The Secret of DevOps: It's Always Been About People, Not Technology," I unveiled what I consider the primary features of DevOps.

In his article, Adam reminded us, *"Becoming better at building and delivering software is the stake. It's not an optional piece of their strategy: It's the future of how their customers want to work with them. Software is table stakes for survival."*

He added, *"But the real answer lies in looking at what John, Paul, and Jesse were doing in 2009—not in the specific technical choices they made, but the style in which they worked, the essence of what they believed made them high functioning and successful. ... Then the challenge begins: how to apply this new style to businesses trying to become better at building and delivering software."*

"DevOps is about bringing together all the people you need to build and run your business effectively, and empowering them to move as quickly as possible toward their goals. Tools matter. Make no mistake: Trying to change the way you work without changing the mechanisms by which you do that work is a futile exercise in excruciating failure."

He concluded, *"Fundamentally, it is about taking the behaviors and beliefs that draw us together as people, combining them with a deep understanding of our customers' needs, and using that knowledge to ship better products to our customers."*

With Respect to Techies, DevOps is Primarily a Business Operational Model

"If you paid attention to what Adam Jacob reported about Jesse, John and Paul's vision, you probably noticed that it emphasizes two fundamental elements of high-performing businesses: the well-known IT infrastructure and the unknown operational model," I told the audience.

Moving to the next slide, I provided evidences to my point, *"As the picture shows, DevOps, according to its founding fathers, isn't the CD platform, automation toolchain or the platform-as-a-service (PaaS) infrastructure solution vendors and certain consultants would like you to believe."*

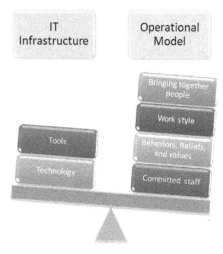

Figure 73 - The Founding Fathers' Vision

The slide seemed to clear up a doubt about what the audience had been hearing. I confirmed, *"With all due respect to my fellow techies, as I've been implementing it, DevOps transcends software development issues; it's a business operational model supporting your company's competitiveness."*

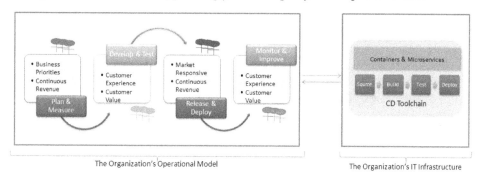

Figure 74 - DevOps as the Business Value Chain

I told the audience I chose to represent it as a two-component system *"because I wanted to make sure IT professionals and business leaders understand that implementing DevOps is primarily a business transformation effort for optimizing the organization's operational model and IT infrastructure."*

I added, *"The operational model is the subset of interactions, staff and skills, processes and practices, values and beliefs, and tools that's repeatedly mobilized across your organization to generate the expected business benefits. It's where all its value propositions and competitive*

---

advantages—organizational agility, flexibility and velocity, innovation culture, more like it—are created."

As (fellow speaker) Stephanie Carton puts it, *"the operational model is where DevOps culture is implemented."*

Anticipating the audience's reaction to that point, I said, *"It doesn't mean CD toolchains are useless or doesn't bring value, without them we're dead. The point here is, business benefits result from an optimized operational model enabled by a well-engineered CD toolchain."*

I'm not the first one to go against the techie perspective of DevOps, I warned. *"Ernest Mueller in his fantastic, "DevOps: It's Not Chef and Puppet," raised the red flag."* His message is clear: *"If someone has a systems problem, and you say that the answer to that problem is Chef or Puppet, you understand neither the problem nor the tools."*

The Near Future of DevOps

In the first part of this article, I wanted to share with you the clarifications I made and more importantly, re-establish the truth on messages as erroneous as *"DevOps means CD toolchain and Agile practices,"* and *"CD infrastructure or software development on its own creates business value."*

They're misleading CIOs and are taking hundreds of projects straight into the wall!

The Key Takeaways

This what I wanted to tell you about DevOps as we discussed it. The key takeaways are:

- DevOps isn't narrowed to agile practices and CD toolchains. Don't fall into the trap of certain solution vendors who tell you that Git, Jenkins, Cucumber, Chef, Containers and microservices will boost your business performance. It's false; things aren't that simplistic.
- DevOps combines an optimized operational model and a CD platform to bring together marketing, sales, post sales, software development, testing and operations into an application delivery capability that boosts your organization's competitiveness.
- Starting the CD toolchain implementation without optimizing the operational model is the surest way to take your DevOps implementation project into the wall.

- DevOps implementation is primarily a business transformation effort, not just an IT capability deployment effort

What matters isn't applications and digital services delivery at the speed of light, but the timely delivery of added-value applications and digital services to the right market segments and business users.

According to Econocom's feedback, most participants are reviewing their DevOps implementation strategy; they will make their operational model optimization the priority.

Mission accomplished!

Appendix C – The Future of the CIO, The Future of Work

Published on CIO.com in 2015, this article went viral and was praised by many observers of the IT industry as a major contribution to the debate on the future of the CIO, and more importantly, on the future of work.

....

In recent years business lines have been increasingly going the shadow IT route to achieve their critical objectives, showing there's a real disconnect with IT as to how to leverage cloud computing.

The problem lies with cloud vendors who ignore the issue of the business vision. They see low IT costs and accelerated application delivery as business growth drivers while businesses are more concerned with market responsiveness achieved through agile and collaborative environments that bring together the business and IT.

The business is right: organizational silos, hierarchical barriers, unclear business priorities and people issues like power struggles, resistance to change, defiance of policies and politics are all impediments that only make it more difficult to achieve flexibility, fast problem solving and decision making.

The solution is to implement IT-as-a-Service (ITaaS) in the form of integrated platforms of people, processes, practices, governance structure and tools specifically built to bring the business and IT together.

The business facet of the digital revolution is what matters

The digital revolution which get so much buzz is incompletely explained to CIOs. What they must understand is, to succeed, businesses need to implement integrated digital strategies.

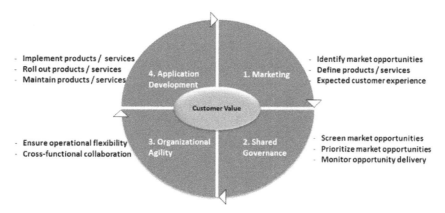

Figure 75 - Integrated Digital Strategy

As Figure 52 shows, what matters most is to increase customer value, not the extensive automation of application deployment suggested by techies.

In fact the business belief is customer value (what customers spend to buy services) results from the organizational dynamics where through a shared governance, IT addresses the opportunities prioritized by marketing, and leverages organizational agility and accelerated application deployment mechanisms to continuously deliver added-value services.

The importance of ITaaS delivery models

The above perspective is accepted in the industry.

VMware and EMC even designate ITaaS as the model through which to implement it. Yet, an overall framework clarifying its principles, organizational and operational implications as well as its deployment practices is still missing.

Most consultants and vendors remain stuck in a techie mindset in which business concerns are at the periphery, not the core. The solution rests on the principles of frameworks like the Complete ITaaS Delivery Model which seeks to increase customer value through three fundamental drivers: the Cloud Platform, the Cloud Services and the IT Operating Model, as shown in Figure 53.

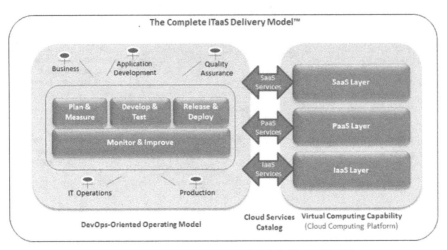

Figure 76 - The Complete ITaaS Delivery Model

The logic is, increasing customer value isn't as simplistic as delivering applications at the speed of light through automated IT processes; rather, it's part of a virtuous circle that spans effective marketing, accelerated application deployment and, most importantly, organizational efficiency improvement. In his best-seller ***Reengineering the Corporation***, former MIT computer science professor Michael M. Hammer warned, "*automating a mess yields an automated mess.*"

What's needed is authentic cloud services from vendors that guarantee, via clear SLAs, available, reliable and scalable IT resources, consumable in a self-service and on-demand manner. They release operational latitudes that create the conditions for organizational agility.

Similarly, the organization's operating model's elements – including people, processes, practices, tools and governance structure – must be arranged in a way that creates operational agility.

Without it, market responsiveness is a wishful thinking.

Key steps CIOs must take to align their IT to ITaaS

One of the reasons digital transformation remains an "elusive mystique" as Joe McKendrick calls it in his must-read "The Elusive Mystique of The Digital Enterprise," is IT players including the major IT vendors are stuck in short-term goals.

They lack the big picture vision and don't understand how cloud solutions, operating models and cloud services combine to generate customer value. Following are three key steps you can take to align your IT to ITaaS.

Reinvent your CIO role, think beyond technology

The disconnect with the business has reached a tipping point, as the use of shadow IT demonstrates. By legitimizing the idea that technology is the only business growth driver, IT vendors have confined CIOs to the limited role of IT tools provider.

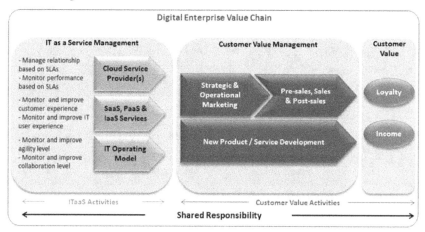

Figure 77 - The Digital Enterprise Value Chain

To win legitimacy the CIO must trade his tools provider jacket for that of business strategy facilitator. As Figure 54 shows, he must contribute to his organization's Digital Enterprise Value Chain (a set of added-value activities) by focusing on IT as a Service Management activities.

Develop the vision of your future Virtual Computing Capability (VCC) and unlock the cloud's cost savings

Taking your IT organization to ITaaS involves converting your datacenter into the VCC that'll cut your IT costs and streamline your IT processes, as Figure 55 demonstrates.

Discuss with your IT teams the following issues:

- The workload to migrate including applications, software and hardware configurations as well as security, backup, disaster recovery and fault tolerance requirements
- The overall architecture of your VCC, particularly the IaaS layer that'll serve as the cost-effective Virtual Infrastructure and the PaaS layer that'll implement a continuous delivery platform to enable accelerated application delivery

- Operational management and executive control of the overall VCC

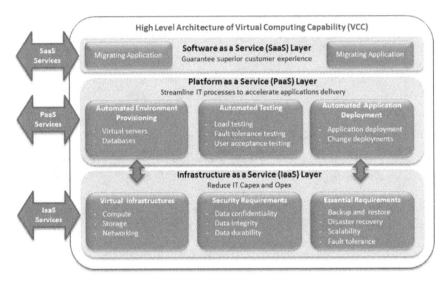

Figure 78 - The Virtual Computing Capability (VCC)

Rethink collaboration with the business, institutionalize DevOps to remove the impediments to operational flexibility and make your IT agile

For years essential value drivers like organizational and operational consistency, shared governance, executive consensus and cross-functional collaboration have been ignored.

Whether techies admit it or not, poor IT focus on priorities, organizational dysfunctions, poor policy adoption and the like are the primary impediments to value and they aren't fixed by technology.

When not narrowed to improving communication between application development and IT operations and to automating application deployment processes, DevOps is the agile and collaborative platform to adopt.

Extended to business issues, its principles, processes and practices simplify the organization's collaboration network and accelerate prioritization and decision-making, helping to make the operating model agile.

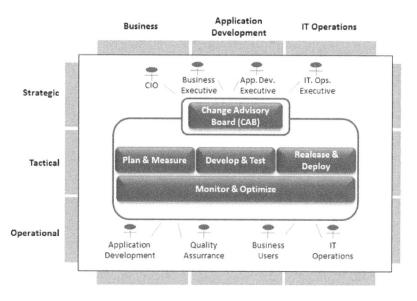

Figure 79 - **Extended DevOps-based IT Operating Model**

Set up an ITaaS task force involving the business and IT to discuss the following issues:

- Establishment of an extended DevOps structure that's not only focused on application development but spans the overall enterprise digital strategy (EDS) activities
- Alignment of DevOps principles, practices, processes and tools to your business considerations
- Establishment of a change advisory board (CAB) serving as shared governance to identify priorities, create consensus on them and provide executive leadership to facilitate their delivery
- Establishment of a continuous delivery platform providing the logic and the infrastructure needed to accelerate application delivery

Wrapping up

To help their business grow and prosper in the digital economy, CIOs must reinvent their IT with ITaaS. The widely spread notion that cloud solutions on their own will make IT organizations agile and boost business growth is an intellectual swindle which not only keeps them in the now outdated role of IT tools provider but also widens the gap between the business and IT.

In his article, *"Cloud Computing's Second Act is All Business,"* Joe McKendrick warns, "IT is one small piece of the cloud story. A much bigger story is coming from the business itself. This is also the hard part." IT vendors that purposely tell a different story aren't helping.

Bibliography

Creating Shared Value – Michael E. Porter and Mark R. Kramer

Four Superpowers to Outperform in the Network Economy – Kevin Echraghi from FABERNOVEL

GAFA: How to be Part of this Network Economy – Barbara Chazelle from Meta-Media

GAFAnomics: A New Economy Wrapping the Planet (Part 1) – Kevin Echraghi from FABERNOVEL

GAFAnomics companies operate as Networks (Part 2) – Kevin Echraghi from FABERNOVEL

Five Stages in the Design Thinking Process – The Interaction Design Foundation

How to Become a Networked Company to Win a World Dominated by GAFAnomics? – Kevin Echraghi from FABERNOVEL

Innovation by Design – Thomas Lockwood and Edgar Papke

Platform Revolution – Geoffrey Parker, Marshall W. Van Alstyne, and Sangeet Paul Choudary

Strategies for Two-Sided Markets – Thomas Eisenmann, Geoffrey Parker, and Marshall W. Van Alstyne

The Phoenix Project – Gene Kim, Kevin Behr, and George Spafford

The DevOps Handbook – Gene Kim, Jez Humble, Patrick Debois, and John Willis

Wikipedia Encyclopedia – Free encyclopedia written collaboratively by the people who use it

Index

111, 112, 113, 114, 115, 116,
117, 118, 119